# Edge of Time

# Edge of Time

## Traveling in Armenia and Karabagh

### Second Edition

Matthew Karanian
Robert Kurkjian

Stone Garden Productions

Washington, DC

4

This second edition published June 2002 by Stone Garden Productions, Washington, DC and Northridge, California. Previous edition published June 2001.

Printed in the United States of America

10 9 8 7 6 5 4 3 2

Library of Congress Control Number 2002091874

ISBN 0-9672120-2-2   19.95

The publisher and authors have made every effort to make the information in this travel guide as accurate as possible. However, they accept no responsibility for any loss, injury or inconvenience sustained by anyone using this book.

Photographs

Images in this guide are available for licensing and also as original fine art prints from Stone Garden Productions / www.StoneGardenProductions.com / info@stonegardenproductions.com / 1-888-266-7331. For additional images, please visit www.KurkjianImages.com

Cover: Karmravor Church, located just outside Yerevan in the town of Ashtarak, and (inset) Khor Virap Monastery, © 2002 R. Kurkjian.

The authors acknowledge Mr. Sarkis Acopian and the American University of Armenia for generously giving permission to use maps originally produced for the Birds of Armenia project.

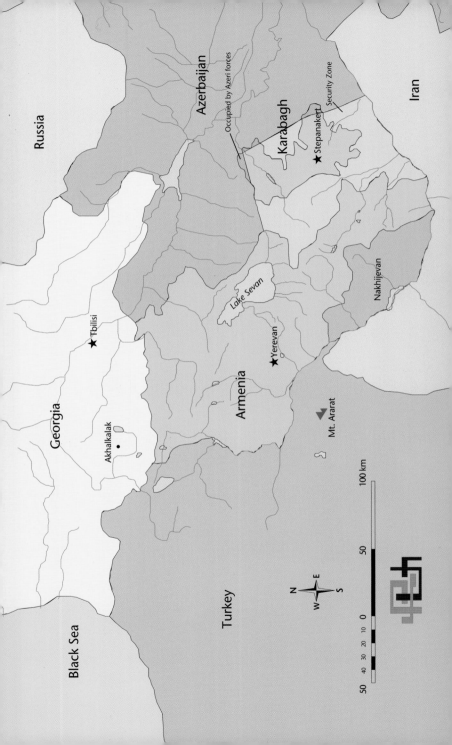

Dedicated to those who
have fought and suffered
for an independent
Armenian homeland.

# CREATING THIS TRAVEL GUIDE

The authors have each lived and worked in Armenia and Karabagh since 1995, and this book is a product of their countless miles of excursions to the most remote reaches of the region. Their research is original, and when the authors recommend a site, or suggest a travel route, it's because they've been there, and they know the best—and the worst—way to go. They've flown to Armenia through all the major European hubs, and they've traveled the countryside by bus, van and car. The authors haven't stayed in every hotel, but they've visited each one and verified every hotelier's claim. If they name a restaurant or café, you can be sure that they've eaten there and are offering first-hand observations and recommendations. These are things you cannot do in a couple of weeks. They did them over the course of several years.

Matthew Karanian wrote all of the unsigned material, and edited the text. He also did the original research for this edition. Robert Kurkjian was the photography editor, and he created the form of this book. He also contributed original research. Vicken Yegparian served as editorial consultant. He verified facts, proofread the text, and assisted with the transliteration of Armenian words. Jim Hulsman of Creative Images (818-887-5271) served as design consultant and he oversaw the layout for this edition.

## TRANSLITERATION

The names of the people and places appearing in this book have generally been transliterated into the Latin alphabet based on the Eastern Armenian pronunciations. Exceptions are made and transliterations based upon Western Armenian pronunciation are used when the Western Armenian transliteration is more widely recognized.

## PRICES

We have listed prices in Armenian dram, with a parenthetical reference to the US dollar equivalent, whenever payment is expected in Armenian currency. Prices are listed in US dollars, without reference to the dram equivalent, when payment is expected to be made in American currency. One dollar is worth roughly 565 dram. Other currencies, including the Russian ruble, are not in general circulation in Armenia or Karabagh and they are therefore not included in this book.

## OMISSIONS

Every guidebook must be selective when deciding what to list. Omission is not necessarily a criticism, and may occur for reasons unrelated to the quality of the shop, hotel or museum. In some cases, it is simply necessary to place a limit upon the number of similar entries that can be included, in order to avoid needless repetition. If you have comments about what is printed, or if you have information to add or correct, we invite your correspondence. This will help us to make improvements in subsequent editions. We prefer to receive correspondence by e-mail: info@StoneGardenProductions.com. You may also write to us at: Stone Garden Productions; 4501 Connecticut Ave., NW; Suite 1112; Washington, DC 20008.

# CONTENTS

10

*Photograph on page 2: Villager at Dadi Vank monastery, M. Karanian.*
*Photograph on page 6:  Man praying at Genocide Memorial in Yerevan, M. Karanian.*

# PREFACE

Their stories have become familiar to us. A traveler visits Armenia for the first time. The purpose might be to visit a family. Or to get closer to family roots. Or perhaps the visitor plans to build a new business, or to rebuild an ancient church.

The reasons for the visit are many. But the expectations are few. The visitor expects, in some small way, to make Armenia a better place.

What we have seen, however, is that it's the visitor who always gets the better deal. It's always the traveler who leaves Armenia a better person.

Why?

Perhaps it's easier to improve one person than it is to rebuild an entire nation. Or perhaps the changes in the individual are merely easier to see. But these answers are probably too simplistic. The answer, instead, can be found in the heart of the Armenian nation.

The modern republic of Armenia was born only a decade ago, but the history of the Armenian nation is more than 3,000 years old. Armenia has survived against long odds, and it has persevered despite apparent futility. The Roman Empire thrived, and then crumbled, while ruling—nominally—the distant lands of Armenia. Byzantine, Persian and Arab Empires have come and gone, but Armenia has always remained.

"The impression is that history had no beginning in Armenia—it has always existed," writes the novelist Andrei Bitov in *A Captive of the Caucasus,* a book that expresses his improbable love affair with Armenia. "There is probably no village that was not, in days of old, the capital of an ancient state, no hill around which a decisive battle has not raged, no stone not moistened with blood, and no man to whom this is a matter of indifference."

Visitors to Armenia are quickly overpowered by the quiet grandeur of this struggle, and by the character of the people who undertake it. The result, often, is visitors who travel to Armenia to learn about their roots, and who return home having learned far more about themselves.

But even without being introspective you are still certain to be awed by Armenia. Forget the old gray images you may have seen of a country ravaged by war and repressed by Communism. This is a land of stunning beauty. Endless poppies create swaths of red across the horizon. Snow-capped mountains stretch toward the sky. Alpine lakes beckon brave swimmers, and rolling hills invite hikers and adventurers. We were so delighted by the color and drama of Armenia's landscape that we featured it prominently in *Out of Stone: Armenia-Artsakh,* our photography book that celebrates this land and its people.

One of the most common responses that the public has had to our images is surprise. "I never realized Armenia was so beautiful," we are often told. Well, neither did we, until we took to the roads and traveled the countryside.

During our travels around Armenia, we have often felt that we were standing at the edge of time, at the frontier between past and present, between antiquity and modernity. At times we felt that we were teetering at this edge, at risk of being devoured by three millennia of tradition.

If Armenia could speak, perhaps it could help us understand how it maintains its balance. Perhaps Armenia would tell us, as Bitov discovered for himself, that it lives somewhere between the past and the present, in hope of a future.

The essence of Armenia is distilled from its ancient past, and for an eternity, Armenia seemed to dwell there, as well. Now for the first time in centuries there's a sun, and not a storm, on its horizon, and the nation once again has an opportunity to thrive. What an exciting time this is to travel in Armenia! We wonder how quickly Armenia will modernize and move forward. We wonder whether it might instead remain tradition-bound. But regardless of the path that Armenia chooses, it will always remain in our hearts as a nation at the *Edge of Time*.

*Matthew Karanian*
*Robert Kurkjian*

M. Karanian                                    *Monastery of Marmashen, near Gyumri*

# Essentials

## PLANNING YOUR TRIP

Armenia and Karabagh are two of the most homogenously populated places on Earth. Roughly 95 percent of the population in each country is ethnic Armenian, and almost everyone reads and writes in the Armenian language and is a member of the Armenian Apostolic Church. The two countries use the same currency, and have strong cultural and social ties, owing to their common ancestry. It is natural, therefore, to cover both states in one travel guide.

Most travelers don't make it any farther than Armenia, however, and many more don't have the time to travel far beyond the capital area of Yerevan. We have highlighted the information accordingly, but we have included basic information on the remote destinations so that visitors can properly plan itineraries for vacations or business trips lasting from one week to one month.

The tourism infrastructure of Armenia and Karabagh is in its formative stages. This means that you are not likely to encounter crowds of tourists here. It also means that a journey here should probably be characterized as an adventure and not as a routine vacation. If you seek them out, there are enough Western-style comforts to prevent you from feeling deprived. The decision for you to make is therefore not *whether* to have an adventure, but rather *what kind* of adventure to have. Use this guide to help you select the adventure that's right for you.

## WHEN TO GO

**Autumn** weather in Armenia and Karabagh is great, making this the best season for travel. Temperatures are moderate and there aren't too many rainy days, even in the mountainous regions. **Spring** arrives in mid-March in many parts of Armenia, and by April you can get by with just a light coat or sweater. You'll also need an umbrella on many days, however, and in Karabagh you should plan on plenty of fog and drizzle. **Summer** is sunny and dry. The days can get hot and parched, especially in Yerevan and the Ararat Valley, so if this is when you plan to travel, you will need to take precautions against dehydration and excessive exposure to the sun. You will want to avoid traveling during **winter**, which runs from December through February. The weather can get cold and snowy.

There are no times of the year when throngs of tourists clog facilities and cause delays and annoyances. At Armenia's Lake Sevan, however, the best hotel facilities usually have no vacancies in August.

## Holidays and Special Events

Armenia has two **Independence Day** holidays, both of which are significant, but neither is as festive as the Fourth of July or Bastille Day. Armenia celebrates the anniversary of its 1918 independence on May 28, and the anniversary of its 1991 re-establishment of independence on September 21. The most significant holiday for all Armenians is **Armenian Genocide Memorial Day**, on April 24. This is a national day of mourning, and a visit at this time would give added significance to your journey. There is a list of major Armenian holidays in the Appendix.

# GETTING THERE

Getting to Armenia and Karabagh is a relatively simple, although tiring, matter. There are several commercial flights to Armenia each week, and there's reliable ground transportation to Karabagh from Armenia. Because of the time difference, flights to Armenia from the US arrive two mornings after departure. The lost time is made up on the return flight, when the morning flight out of Yerevan arrives in the US later that same day.

## Before You Go

A **passport** and **visa** are required. Passports must be valid for at least six months beyond the date of entry to the country. In the US, a visa can be obtained from the Consular Section of the Armenian Embassy, 2225 R Street, NW, Washington, DC 20008 (Tel. 202-319-2983), or from the Consulate General of Armenia in California at 50 N. La Cienega Blvd., Suite 210, Beverly Hills, CA 90211 (Tel. 310-657-6102). Reception hours at the Consular Section of the embassy in Washington are 10 am until noon each weekday except Wednesday. Reception hours in Los Angeles are 9:30 AM until 1:30 PM daily. For Armenian embassies in countries other than the US, refer to the list at the end of this section.

Three-week **tourist visas** are relatively simple to obtain. There's a short application form that is available by mail or online at **www.armeniaemb.org**. The fee is $60 and the processing time is seven business days. Faster processing is available for an additional fee.

Travelers who wish to stay more than three weeks must obtain a letter of invitation from a resident of Armenia. For a **90-day business visa**, the letter of invitation must be sent directly to the Consular Department of the Ministry of Foreign Affairs in Yerevan. For a **90-day tourist visa**, the letter of invitation must be sent directly to the Passport and Visa Department of the Ministry of Internal Affairs in Yerevan. The consular section of the embassy will provide particulars on how to file these letters and it will process the paperwork and issue the visa. The cost is $35 for a single-entry visa and $65 for a multiple-entry visa. Full details on other types of visas are available on the Armenian Embassy's website or directly from the embassy in Washington, DC.

Business travelers who intend to reside in Armenia for more than three months must obtain a **residency permit** from the Ministry of Internal Affairs after their arrival in

Armenia. Please see the section on Business Travelers for more information about this requirement.

Travelers from the US must now obtain a separate national visa for each of the Newly Independent States that they intend to visit. Three-day **transit visas** are usually offered, and a three-day visa to Armenia is available for only $18. If you are planning to take a weekend trip to Georgia during your visit to Armenia, keep in mind that a standard tourist visa permits only one entry into Armenia. If you intend to cross the border into Armenia more than once, you will need one of those 90-day visas, which requires a letter of invitation, as described above. The alternative is to get a new Armenia visa from the Armenian Embassy in Georgia before you return. If you're returning to Armenia from Karabagh, this restriction is not enforced.

If you need to overstay your visa, you can get an extension from the Ministry of Internal Affairs. If you attempt to leave Armenia with an **expired visa**, you will be assessed a fine of $3 for each day that you overstay.

## Travel Information

The US Dept. of State provides Travel Warnings and Consular Information Sheets on all countries, including Armenia (Tel. 202-647-5225; Fax 202-647-3000) (Internet: www.state.gov). For emergency information about an American traveling overseas, call the Office of Overseas Citizens Services (Tel. 202-647-5225). The Dept. of State characterizes the relationship between Armenia and the US as "excellent," and points out that the US Embassy was the first embassy to open in Yerevan in February 1992. "It is not likely," says their most recent commercial guide to Armenia, "that civil disturbances, if they occur, would be directed against US businesses or the US community." Most travelers also report that Americans and other Westerners are generally well liked and warmly received. There are also travel advisories that are intended specifically for citizens of Canada (Tel. 800-267-6788; 613-944-6788) (Internet: www.voyage.gc.ca) and of the UK (Tel. 20-7008-0232) (Internet: www.fco.gov.uk).

## Maps

You may wish to have a detailed map before you go to Armenia so that you can plan your itinerary. The Birds of Armenia project (Internet: www.aua.am/boa) has an excellent map of Armenia and Map Link has a detailed road map of all of the southern Caucasus. Each costs roughly $10 and is available by mail order from most of the bookstores listed in the Appendix.

## Customs

There have been significant reforms of customs procedures in Armenia during the past few years, resulting in a painless procedure for most travelers. It's no longer necessary to write down every item you carry in, such as your wedding band or your wristwatch. But it has been routine during the past few years for customs officers to x-ray all baggage. There is no limit upon the amount of Armenian or foreign

Essentials

currency that can be brought in or out of the country. Transfers of $10,000 or more are subject to reporting requirements according to Armenian law, however, and the transfer must be made electronically. US law obligates travelers who enter or depart the US while carrying $10,000 or more in US currency to file a declaration with the US Customs office.

Travelers who carry rare or expensive items into the country, and who intend to carry them back out, should declare these items upon their arrival. You will be given a form that you must present to customs upon your departure, so that you may avoid an export tax. Commercial goods (items fresh from the factory that look like you might sell them) that exceed $500 in value are taxable. Personal items are excluded from this calculation.

There are no restrictions on the type of food that may be imported, but quantity limits are imposed on many items, unless you have an import license. There's a 20-pack import and export limit on cigarettes, a 2-liter limit on alcohol, and a 1-kilogram limit on coffee. There is an absolute prohibition on the import or export of pornography, drugs and explosives. Prescription medicine should be left in its original drug store container, with a note from your doctor if you are carrying a large quantity.

Customs officers are trained to look for carpets, paintings and antiquities when travelers are departing the country. Exporting antiquities with cultural or historic value is restricted. If you intend to export any item that is, or might be mistaken for, an antique, then you should apply for a special license at the Ministry of Culture. Without this license, you should expect that your carpet will be seized. Either obtain the license from the merchant, or apply in person at the Ministry of Culture, 5 Tumanian Street (Tel. 55-19-20). When you return to the US you will not be permitted to bring food products through Customs.

*M. Karanian*                                                      *Sarsang Reservoir, Karabagh*

## Selected Armenian Embassies

**United States:** 2225 R Street, NW; Washington, DC 20008. (Tel. 202-319-1976). Additional office, consulate only, at 50 N. La Cienega Blvd., Suite 210, Beverly Hills, Calif. 90211 (Tel. 310-657-6102) www.armeniaemb.org

**Canada:** 7 Delaware Ave., Ottawa, Ontario K2P 0Z2 (Tel. 613-234-3710)

**France:** 9 Rue Viete, 75017 Paris (Tel. 331-4-212-9800)

**Georgia:** 4 Tetelashvilis Kucha; Tbilisi (Tel. 32-959-443)

**Great Britain:** 25A Cheniston Gardens, London, England W8 6TG (Tel. 011-44-20-7938-5435)

**Iran:** 1 Ostad Shahriar; Teheran (Tel. 982-1-670-833; 982-1-670-4833)

**Russia:** Armianski Pereulok 2; Moscow (Tel. 095-924-1269)

Armenia also maintains embassies or consulates in Argentina, Austria, Belarus, Bulgaria, Egypt, Germany, Greece, India, Iraq, Italy, Kazakhstan, Lebanon, Romania, Switzerland, Syria, Turkmenistan, and Ukraine.

## Selected Foreign Embassies

**United States:** 18 Baghramian Ave. (Tel. 52-46-61; 52-16-11) Ambassador: John Ordway; Deputy Chief of Mission: Patricia Moller. There are plans to move the embassy, perhaps in 2003 or 2004, to a location at the edge of the city (Internet: www.arminco.com/embusa/consul.htm)

**Canada:** 25/22 Demirjian Street. Consulate only. (Tel. 56-79-03)

**France:** 8 Grigor Lusavorich Street, behind Republic Square (Tel. 56-11-03; 15-15-93) (Internet: www.ambafran.am)

**Georgia:** 42 Arami Street, near Abovian Street (56-13-67; 58-55-11)

**Germany:** 29 Charents Street (Tel. 58-65-91; 56-91-85)

**Great Britain:** 28a Charents Street (Tel. 55-30-81)

**Iran:** 1 Budaghian Street, near Komitas Ave. (Tel. 52-98-30; 22-33-40) (Internet: www.iranembassy.am)

**Russia:** 13 Grigor Lusavorich Street (Tel. 58-24-63; 56-16-92)

Several other nations also have embassies in Armenia, including China, Egypt, Greece, India, Iraq, Lebanon, Romania, Syria and Ukraine.

## Getting There by Air

Most Western travelers arrive in Armenia by air at Yerevan's Zvartnots Airport. The only other commercial airport in Yerevan, Erebuni Airport, is intended for domestic flights, but is not now in use. Zvartnots Airport is about 17 km from Yerevan, and the 20-minute cab ride should not cost more than $10 to $12 unless you're traveling with a group or have excess luggage. There's a bus that makes the journey, too, but departure times are not reliable.

The state airline, **Armenian Airlines** (www.armenianairlines.am), once held a monopoly on flights into the capital from the West, but it has faced tough times lately. It surrendered its monopoly a few years ago and began sharing its Europe-to-Yerevan routes with several major carriers. The competition has lowered fares. Depending upon the season, round trip airfares from the US are now between $800 and $1,500.

This airline once operated routes into Yerevan from most major European cities, but by mid-2002 it appeared that they would all be cancelled owing to its lack of aircraft that meet international standards for noise, safety and pollution. For the latest flight information, call them in Yerevan (Tel. 22-75-32; 22-54-47). Their cutback follows the lead of **Swiss Air**, which discontinued its Zurich-to-Yerevan route in 2001.

**VG Airlines** (www.vgair.be) (Tel. 32-3-303-00-00), a new airline that is based in Belgium, hopes to fill the gap. This airline started its operations in early 2002, after purchasing aircraft from the defunct Sabena Airlines. It plans to begin operating a direct Los Angeles to Yerevan flight, with only a one-hour stopover in Brussels. If it is operated properly, this 16-hour flight on an Airbus A330 could become the easiest way to reach Armenia from Los Angeles. Schedules and prices had not yet been established when this book was printed.

**British Airways** (www.britishairways.com) (Tel. 800-247-9297) is now the leading carrier offering service to Armenia. The airline offers flights from London to Yerevan, with a 45-minute stopover in Tbilisi. BA's partner, British Mediterranean, actually operates the flight, using BA planes and personnel, and the airline offers the flight three times weekly, usually on a modern Airbus A320. In 2002, scheduled flights departed London on Mondays, Wednesdays and Fridays. Return flights from Yerevan departed on Saturdays, Tuesdays and Thursdays. The BA office in Yerevan is located at 10 Sayat Nova Ave. (Tel. 52-12-83; 52-82-20).

**Aeroflot** (www.aeroflot.com) (Tel. 888-340-6400) provides service through Moscow, but travelers have reported difficulties making transfers at the Moscow airport. They're located in Yerevan at 12 Mesrop Mashtots Ave. **Austrian Airlines** (www.austrianair.com) (Tel. 800-843-0002) also has three weekly flights to Yerevan.

**Sidon Travel** specializes in arranging flights from the US to Armenia, and can often book a seat for a fare that is lower than the airlines. They can be reached at 5825 Sunset Blvd., Suite 218; Hollywood, CA (Tel. 323-466-9161; 800-826-7960). **Levon Travel** is also an Armenia travel specialist. Located at 1132 North Brand Blvd., Glendale, CA (Tel. 818-552-7700).

Flights from European hubs are all red-eyes. Departure times are generally in the evening, and the flights do not arrive in Yerevan until the following morning. Connecting flights into Europe from the US follow the same schedule, which means that by the time you finally arrive in Armenia, you will have spent two full nights in the air, and a full day of layover at an airport in Europe. After such a marathon of travel, you probably won't want to schedule too many activities for your first day in Armenia. To make the journey more pleasant, you should include a toothbrush and some other toiletries in your carry-on luggage so that you can freshen up between flights.

## Getting There Overland

The only overland route to Armenia that an American can conveniently take is through the Republic of Georgia, which is located to the north. Armenia's borders with Turkey and Azerbaijan are closed and militarized. Armenia's border with Iran is open, but crossing from Iran probably wouldn't be comfortable for someone traveling on a US passport.

Buses make a daily run between Tbilisi, Georgia, and Yerevan, but the cheap 3,000-dram (about $6) fare is made less enticing by the painful six-to-eight-hour ride on an old run-down heap. A small van, generally one that is in good condition, operates on the same route twice daily. The fare is 6,000 dram (about $12), and travel time is only about four or five hours. Buses arrive in Yerevan at the Kilikia Central Bus Station on Admiral Isakov Ave., but the driver will often discharge passengers in the center of the city, as well, in exchange for a gratuity.

When making the crossing in a car, you can expect to be scrutinized by border guards on both the Georgian and Armenian sides. It may sometimes be necessary to offer a modest "grease" payment of $10 in order to expedite the process. This is usually enough to put everything in order and to get you on your way.

## Arriving and Leaving

The US Embassy encourages US citizens to register their presence. You don't have to do this, but if you do it will make it easier for the embassy staff to locate you in an emergency. To register, stop by the consular office of the embassy in Yerevan. The entrance is located halfway down the driveway on the left side of the embassy building at 18 Baghramian Ave. Whether you register or not, you should make a couple of photocopies of your passport and keep them in a safe place. Having a photocopy will make it easier to get a replacement passport if the original is lost.

At the airport upon your departure from Armenia and before you can check your bags you must pay an airport tax, in Armenian currency, at a special window. The 10,000-dram tax is equivalent to about $20. Plan ahead so that you won't have to change money at the airport.

Essentials

# ONCE THERE

## SAFETY

By mid-2002, the terrorism of September 11 had not had any apparent effect upon the ability to travel safely throughout Armenia. Armenian officials have not reported any new restrictions on travel and Western visitors—particularly Americans and Canadians—are well liked and warmly received. Violent street crime is almost unheard of in Armenia, but hostile relations with Azerbaijan and Turkey make it necessary for travelers to avoid straying close to the frontiers with these countries. The borders are militarized and are well marked, so you need not worry about accidentally entering a dangerous area.

Visitors can probably avoid one of Armenia's greatest nuisances—police stops. This is because tourists are unlikely to have an opportunity to even drive a car in Armenia. Laws require that only the registered owner of a car can be a driver. Throughout the former Soviet Union, it is customary for police to stop drivers without reason, in order to check their "documents." What they're really looking for is money, usually only about 1,000 dram ($2), in exchange for which the driver is allowed to continue on his way. Foreigners generally don't have to pay anything, unless they have actually committed an infraction, but the stops can nevertheless be annoying.

## MONEY

### Armenian Currency

Armenia has a cash economy. Credit cards are not widely accepted outside of the major hotels, and attempting to use them even there can be cumbersome. Visitors should therefore plan to bring enough cash for their entire stay. ATM machines exist, but are rare. Please see the Yerevan chapter for a list of locations.

The local currency is the dram, which was trading in early 2002 at about 565 dram to the dollar. The dram is circulated predominantly in paper notes in denominations of 10, 25, 50, 100, 500, 1000, 5000, 20,000 and 50,000 dram. There are almost no coins in circulation, although a 5-dram coin (worth less than a penny) will sometimes show up in your change when you purchase subway tokens at the metro station. Denominations of 1,000 dram and higher can frequently be difficult to exchange, and the 20,000 dram note, which is the equivalent of about $35, can rarely be negotiated, except at a bank or hotel. Most of the notes have been redesigned during the past three years, and it is not unusual to find two different designs in circulation for the 50 through 1,000-dram values.

### Exchanging Money

The US dollar is widely accepted for larger transactions, but new bills, without marks or tears, are preferred. For most retail purchases, however, you will need to have Armenian dram. You can lawfully exchange dollars, without a commission, from merchants located in post offices, hotels, and even on the street. Dollars are

*Photograph: Waterfall in southern Armenia, near Sisian, M. Karanian*

preferred, but you may also be able to exchange euros and rubles. British currency, however, is more difficult to exchange. Bills should always be new and clean. The worst exchange rates are offered at Yerevan's airport and at the major hotels such as the Hotel Armenia. For the best rates, try any of the shops located along Tigran Mets Ave. in Yerevan, just off Republic Square.

## Exchange Rates

Armenia's currency, the dram, has remained fairly stable for the past several years. These rates, which were current in early 2002, can be used as a guide to what the actual rates will be when you travel. For up-to-the-minute rates for the dram and for every other currency in circulation worldwide, consult **www.xe.com**. The euro and the US dollar are the most popular foreign currencies and you can even find the euro in general circulation in Karabagh.

United States...............................................1 dollar: 565 dram

Europe........................................................1 euro: 495 dram

Russia.........................................................1 ruble: 18 dram

Great Britain...............................................1 pound: 806 dram

Canada.........................................................1 dollar: 357 dram

## TIME

Local time in Armenia and Karabagh is 12 hours ahead of California, nine hours ahead of New York, and four hours ahead of Greenwich Mean Time. When it's 9 am Sunday in Los Angeles, it's already 9 pm in Yerevan. Time changes for daylight savings have not always been made in unison with the rest of the world, however, and so it is possible that the time differences from October through March will be reduced by one hour.

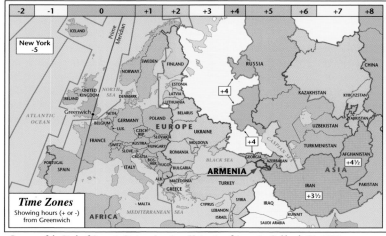

*Courtesy of the Birds of Armenia Project, American University of Armenia, Oakland, CA, 1999*

# MAIL

Mail within Armenia is frequently lost or misdirected, and the post office should not be relied upon for delivering anything in Armenia that you really want to arrive at its destination. You might have better success with the Armenian post office for mail that is to be delivered outside the country. To send a letter or package from Armenia, to a destination outside of Armenia, it is best to mail it from a post office in Yerevan. Private couriers such as FedEx and DHL also operate from Yerevan. Please see the Yerevan chapter for more details.

# ELECTRICITY

Standard voltage in Armenia and Karabagh is 220V. Appliances from the US are designed for 110V, however, so you will need a converter. The voltage sometimes deviates from the standard, so you should also bring a surge protector for computers and other valuable equipment. It may be difficult to find stores in Armenia that sell transformers or surge protectors, so bring these from home. For the past few years, power outages have been uncommon in Armenia. Therefore, back-up power sources are less important than they once were.

Electric outlets use European-style plugs with two round pins. You will therefore need plug adaptors for US appliances, in addition to the voltage converter. These are sold in the US, and they are also readily available in Yerevan at electronics stores.

# GETTING AROUND

A tour of Armenia can easily be arranged independently by hiring a **private driver**. This means finding someone, anyone, with a car and agreeing on a fare. Because of the high unemployment rate, finding a driver is not difficult. Most hotels and tour operators will help you locate someone suitable. The going rate is about 100 dram (twenty cents) for each kilometer traveled.

A private driver to Lake Sevan will usually charge about $30 for a stay of several hours. Other typical fares are: $20 to Garni and Geghard; $20 to Khor Virap monastery; $15-$20 to Echmiadzin, but fares will vary depending upon the type of vehicle used and the length of time one stays at a destination. Most cars will accept three or four passengers. A van will usually accept up to 11 passengers. There are several taxi services that will provide a driver at a reasonable rate. In Yerevan try: **Fito Taxi** (Tel. 54-55-45; 54-45-44); or **Ararat Chauffeur Service** (Tel. 34-41-14).

Road conditions are highly variable. Most roadways outside Yerevan are not lighted, and safety features such as guardrails are used sparingly. As a result, driving on secondary roads at night is difficult and many drivers will prefer to get you back to your hotel before sunset. Armenia's days are long in the summer, so this often means getting home as late as 10 pm. Most of the primary roads have been repaired and repaved during the past few years, however, making intercity travel safer and more convenient.

**Hitchhiking** is generally safe, and it's common among all groups, including even the elderly. We've even seen soldiers and police hitching rides. As a result, rides are easy to get, especially outside Yerevan. The greatest danger is instead from the cars themselves, which usually lack seatbelts and other safety features.

Many **tour operators** offer traditional guided group tours. For a sampling of what's available, contact one of these agents. **Prana Tour**, 18 Kievian Street (Tel. 22-54-88; 27-15-42; Fax 27-31-41) (E-mail: prana@arminco.com); **Tatev Tour Agency**, 45 Komitas Ave. (Tel. 23-18-48; 23-18-58; Fax 15-14-39) (E-mail: tatev@acc.am) (Internet: www.arminco.com/tatev); **Menua**, Sayat Nova Ave, in the lobby of the Ani Plaza Hotel. It might be possible to rent a car without a driver from this agency. There is only one car in the rental fleet (Tel. 52-73-72; Fax 58-39-01) (E-mail: info@menuatours.com) (Internet: www.menuatours.com); **First Travel and Service**, 12/2 Parpetsi Street (Tel. 53-40-24; 53-99-01) (E-mail: first@megacom.am); **Tourism Management, Ltd.**, 29 Komitas Ave., 2nd floor (Tel. 22-41-11; Fax 27-73-44) (E-mail: armasta@armasta.am).

Armenian church organizations often sponsor tours, which they advertise as pilgrimages, to Armenia and to historical Armenian areas outside the republic. These are comprehensive tours that must be arranged well in advance. For details contact the **Diocese of the Armenian Church**, 630 Second Ave., New York, NY 10016 (Tel. 212-686-9893; Fax 212-686-0245); or the **Prelacy of the Armenian Apostolic Church**, 138 East 39th Street, New York, NY 10016 (Tel. 212-689-7810).

You may see signs advertising Hertz car rentals in Yerevan, but the cars come with a driver. There are still no big car rental agencies in Armenia where you can rent a car without a driver just as you would in the West. If you plan to live in Armenia and want

*R. Kurkjian*                                          *Foothills of Mt. Aragats, northern Armenia*

to buy a car, you'll need a valid license from your home state and an international driver's license, which you can get from the American Automobile Association in the US. **Bicycles** are not common sights in Armenia, and there aren't any bike rental companies that we know of. If you bring a bicycle to Armenia, the most practical type is a mountain bike, so that you can cover the country's mountainous terrain. Bring spare parts, too. Riding a bicycle in Yerevan can be dangerous because automobile drivers aren't accustomed to seeing and accommodating bicyclists, so use extreme caution.

## PUBLIC TRANSPORTATION

In Yerevan, a **subway** cuts a single swath through the center of the city, and reliably arrives at each station within five minutes of the previous train. Fare is 40 dram (less than ten cents). Local vans operate throughout the city for a fare of 100 dram (about twenty cents). Seating is cramped, and it's not always easy to determine where a particular van will go. Still, at this price, if you end up in the wrong place, at least you won't have to worry about the expense. Cabs are plentiful, but you'll have to find one that's parked. Gasoline is too expensive, and customers too few, for cabbies to drive around looking for fares. A foreigner should expect to pay about 1,000 dram (less than $2) regardless of the destination within the center city. Drivers usually expect a little more for late-night trips. Fares should be negotiated in advance.

For trips between cities, **buses** are available and cheap, but they should be avoided unless you have lots of spare time. Vans are a more expensive, but a safer and faster choice. For a current schedule of both, it's best to check with the bus station one or two days before you intend to travel. Go, in person, to the **Kilikia Central Bus Station**, located on Admiral Isakov Street, for timetables and tickets. Admiral Isakov Street is also known as the Echmiadzin road, because it leads, predictably, to Echmiadzin. The bus station is located just past the Ararat Brandy factory, on the right side of the road.

In addition to service from the bus station, there are several **vans** that depart for **Lake Sevan** from central Yerevan every Saturday and Sunday morning during the summer. Fare is 900 dram (less than $2). The vans depart from the park located near the corner of Sayat Nova Ave. and Moskovian Street, near the Manhattan City Bar. Departure times are when all the seats in a particular van are filled, and generally start around 10 am and conclude by noon. Please see the chapter on Lake Sevan for more information.

### International Travel

Daily vans operate from the Kilikia Central Bus Station to **Stepanakert**, the capital city of **Karabagh**. Departures are at 8 am and at 9 am. Travel time is roughly eight hours and the fare is 6,000 dram (about $11). From Hotel Shirak, a van departs daily at 7:30 am. Travel time is roughly six hours, and the fare is 4,000 dram (about $8). Arrive about an hour before departure so you can select a good seat. A window seat on the right side of the van will provide unobstructed views of Mt. Ararat. To guarantee a seat, buy your ticket the night before. Please see the chapter on Karabagh for more information about traveling to Stepanakert and the surrounding countryside.

Buses and vans operate daily to **Georgia**, but the buses are dreadfully slow and should be avoided. Vans are cleaner, faster, and still reasonably priced. They all depart from Yerevan's Kilikia Central Bus Station, on Admiral Isakov Street. Departures by van to **Tbilisi** are daily at 8 am and again at 9 am. Travel time is only about four or five hours, and the fare is 6,000 dram (about $12). Arrive early to claim a good seat. The actual departure time will be when all the seats are sold. All vehicles arrive in Tbilisi at the **Ortajella Bus Station**. From there, a five-minute cab ride of 8 Georgian lari (about $4) will take you to the center of town. Within Tbilisi, foreign tourists should expect to pay 4 lari (about $2) for just about every fare.

A big and slow bus makes a daily trek to **Akhalkalak**, the Armenian-populated region of Georgia located north of Gyumri, at 9 am. Travel time is at least 8 hours, most of which occurs on the miserable, rocky roads in Georgia. The fare is 1,500 dram (less than $3).

There are no commercial flights scheduled between Yerevan and Tbilisi. British Mediterranean flies from Yerevan to London with a brief stopover in Tbilisi, but the airline does not offer a shuttle between Yerevan and Tbilisi. Travelers between Armenia and Georgia therefore must instead rely upon ground transportation.

A slow bus to **Iran** departs from Hotel Erebuni in Yerevan, for about $50. Check with the Iranian Embassy in Yerevan for visa applications, and to learn about restrictions on travelers who are US citizens. Located at 1 Budaghian Street (Tel. 52-98-30; 28-04-57) (Fax 15-13-85).

There is also a bus to **Turkey** that departs twice weekly from Hotel Erebuni in Yerevan. The bus detours through Georgia in order to avoid the closed Turkish-Armenian border. US citizens can purchase a Turkish visa at the border for about $20. For bus tickets, and to see if the bus is still running, check with **Mahmudoglu Turizm**, Ltd., located at Hotel Erebuni, room 224 (Tel. 56-11-53). If you are in **Istanbul** and wish to travel to Yerevan, call the bus company at their office in Turkey to make arrangements (Tel. 0-212-658-38-34). Armenia does not have an embassy in Turkey, so get your Armenia visa before going to Turkey. There's also another bus line that departs from Yerevan's **Kilikia Central Bus Station** each Wednesday and Saturday that can take you as far as Istanbul. For tickets and schedule information, check with **AST Turizm** Ltd. at their Yerevan office on 50 Nalbandian St. (Tel. 56-44-54).

It is not possible to travel directly to **Azerbaijan**. If your passport contains a Karabagh visa you will certainly be denied entry to Azerbaijan. You might also be arrested, and your safety could be in jeopardy. Do not attempt to travel to Azerbaijan if you have a Karabagh visa in your passport. You will also face difficulties upon seeking entry to Azerbaijan if your passport contains an Armenian visa, or if you have an Armenian surname, although the Azerbaijan Embassy in the US officially denies this.

# HEALTH

Traveling to developing countries such as Armenia and Karabagh presents travelers with the burden of anticipating medical needs that might arise during their visit. Medical supplies are often limited, and if serious needs arise, the patient's familiar network of medical providers won't be able to help.

For the latest information about the precautions you should take before traveling, contact the Centers for Disease Control (CDC), National Center for Infectious Diseases, and ask for their Travelers' Health Bulletin (Tel. 888-232-3299) (Internet: www.cdc.gov/travel). Health advisories for worldwide destinations, including Armenia, are available from the **CDC hotline** (Tel. 404-332-4559). This is the best source for health advisories on all worldwide destinations.

Many communities in the US offer special clinics for overseas travelers where you can get travel immunizations. Check with your local Department of Health. A private professional organization that can help you locate a travel clinic is the International Society of Travel Medicine, PO Box 871089, Stone Mountain, Georgia 30087 USA (Tel. 770-736-7060) (E-mail: istm@mediaone.net) (Internet: www.istm.org).

Armenia and Karabagh do not require proof of any vaccinations to gain entry. If you have special health needs, speak to your physician before traveling. Medical providers advise that travelers to Armenia should have current immunizations for **Diphtheria, Tetanus, Typhoid,** and **Hepatitis A**. The risk of contracting tuberculosis is low, and there is a minimal risk of malaria, but travelers should ideally be vaccinated for **Hepatitis B** if there is a risk you will have contact with blood.

Bring any special medications that you reasonably believe you will need, especially **prescription drugs**. Leave your prescriptions in their original, marked containers, and bring enough to last for your entire stay. If you are planning a long stay, and are therefore bringing a large supply, bring a letter of explanation from your doctor. This will help you avoid problems with customs officers who might otherwise be understandably suspicious.

**Medicine** can be purchased at the many pharmacies throughout Yerevan, but their selections are often limited and are unlikely to include exactly what you want. Outside Yerevan, and in Karabagh, you are apt to find even less. Travelers should therefore bring: fever reducers such as ibuprofen, Tylenol® or aspirin, over-the-counter cold remedies, antidiarrheal medications such as Imodium®, and some antibiotics, as well. Use the antibiotics only under direction of a physician.

In the summer, bring sunblock, sunglasses, and a hat to protect yourself from Armenia's intense and relentless sun. Throughout Armenia and Karabagh, find a pharmacy by looking for a sign with the Russian word "Apteka." Sexually transmitted diseases are present here, as they are in every community. Travelers should take appropriate precautions. Condoms may be difficult to locate, and the available brands may be of poor quality. Travelers should bring whatever they need from home.

Food and waterborne **diseases** are the leading cause of illness in travelers. Travelers' diarrhea can be caused by viruses, bacteria, or parasites, all of which are found everywhere and can contaminate food or water. Infections may cause diarrhea and vomiting, fever, or hepatitis. Make sure your food and drinking water are safe. If you develop a condition that persists long after your visit, see a doctor.

In Armenia and Karabagh, drink only bottled water, or water that has been brought to a full boil, and consume only pasteurized dairy products. When at a café or restaurant, remember to avoid ice cubes. Drinking coffee or tea while dining out should not be risky, provided the drinks were made with boiled water. Use caution when purchasing food from street vendors. Fruit that can be peeled is safe, but others should be washed with either bottled or boiled water.

If you are disabled, you should note that most public and private buildings have no special accommodations for wheelchairs, and that many buildings and hotels lack elevators. Check with your hotel or travel agent before booking a room.

## Medical Emergencies

Emergency facilities are limited. For a **medical emergency** in Yerevan call an ambulance by dialing **03**. If you need hospitalization, the Ministry of Health Hospital #4, located at 21 Paronian Street, usually has an English-speaking doctor or nurse on staff. The American Embassy can offer a list of doctors in general practice and also in various specialties (Tel. 52-16-11; Fax 15-15-50). If the Consulate is closed, you can still get help in an emergency at any time of day or night by calling the Embassy switchboard (15-15-51).

**Travel insurance** is available from many providers in the US. Some policies will cover the cost of transportation to a hospital in Europe or the US in a medical emergency. Insurers call this "med-evac" insurance. Check with an insurance agent in your community to learn more.

## Personal Hygiene

For hard-to-locate Western-brand shampoos, deodorants and beauty items, try the cosmetics store on Abovian Street near Republic Square in Yerevan. The products at pharmacies are often limited to Russian imports. For short visits, bring all the toiletries you anticipate needing.

If you wear contact lenses, bring a spare set and all the cleaning solution that you will need, because you will have difficulty finding these. If you wear eyeglasses, bring a spare pair. Women should bring sanitary napkins and any other special items they may need, rather than hope to find their preferred products.

# BUSINESS TRAVEL

Most of the international business activity in the region occurs in Yerevan, and the information here is therefore intended to assist Westerners who are conducting business in Armenia. Many business customs are based on cultural attitudes of the Armenians, and anyone planning to do business in either Armenia or Karabagh is advised to become familiar with them and to be sensitive to local values.

## Business Customs and Communications

Social activity is an integral part of most business dealings, and visitors should expect that negotiations might therefore include many social invitations. Visits to private homes for lengthy dinners are typical, and refusal would be a social gaffe. The exchange of gifts is also common, as are invitations to visit historic sites such as ancient monasteries or fortresses. Refusing an invitation to visit, for example, the Cathedral of Echmiadzin would suggest a lack of interest in Armenian culture, and would likely be interpreted as a sign of disrespect. Foreign business people in the region should expect that deals will take longer to complete, and that developing a friendship with business partners is desirable.

Communications are not as reliable as they are in the West. The telephone infrastructure is poor, and getting a call through can require several attempts. E-mail and the Internet are only as good as the phone system upon which they rely. Mail delivery is sporadic, and lost items are commonplace. For these reasons, you should not always expect a prompt reply to an inquiry. Even when messages do get through, it is unusual to get an immediate reply, although this has improved the past couple of years.

Many business people rely upon private couriers to deliver their mail within Yerevan, and this is a sensible procedure to use for any mail that really must get through. Cellular telephone service, although limited, is now available, and this system is more reliable than the ground lines. There is no service outside the city on the primary provider. Still, if most of your business will be in Yerevan then it may be wise to rent a cell phone during your visit. Please see the Telephone section in the Yerevan Guide chapter for details.

## Laws

Most law is territorial. The laws from home will not follow you around all over the world. Generally, US law is also territorial, and it will not follow Americans overseas. This means that when you are in a foreign country, the laws of that country, and not of the US, are the laws that govern your conduct.

There are many situations, however, when US law will still reach a US citizen overseas. Federal law prohibits Americans from offering bribes to foreign officials in order to get or retain business. This law, which is known as the Foreign Corrupt Practices Act, follows Americans all over the globe and has applications that are broader than its title implies. A US citizen who bribes an Armenian official, in Armenia, regarding an Armenian contract, can be prosecuted in the US. The law makes an exception for "grease" payments, which are made merely to facilitate or expedite the performance of routine government services. Throughout the former Soviet Union, there is a culture of acceptance of these types of payments. But bribery by an American is a criminal offense that is prosecuted by the US Department of Justice. Consult an attorney to learn the nuances of this potentially onerous law.

## Taxes

US citizens must report their worldwide income on their income tax returns. Living and working overseas will not relieve you of this obligation. You may be entitled to special deductions or exclusions, however, if you live and work outside the US for more than one year. The IRS offers a package of forms and instructions for US citizens living abroad. Ask for Publication 776. Write to: IRS Forms Distribution Center, PO Box 25866, Richmond, Virginia 23289 (Internet: www.irs.gov) or consult a tax specialist.

## Citizenship

You cannot be a dual citizen of Armenia and any other country. Article 14 of the Armenian constitution forbids this. By contrast, the US does not prohibit its citizens from becoming citizens of other countries as well. If you engage in acts that are inconsistent with US citizenship, however, you may, under some circumstances, be deemed to have surrendered your citizenship. You should contact an American embassy or consulate to learn the effect upon your US citizenship if, for example, you plan to accept a position in the government or armed forces of a foreign country. Either of those acts might be considered a voluntary act of expatriation with the intent to relinquish citizenship.

Residence abroad, in and of itself, has no effect on US citizenship. Naturalized US citizens do not need to return to the United States periodically to preserve their citizenship. The State Dept. offers guidance on its web site, www.state.gov.

## Special Residency Status

Armenian law permits foreigners to obtain special residency status if they are of ethnic Armenian ancestry or if they are engaged in economic or cultural activities in the country. Successful applicants are granted Armenian national passports which are valid for ten years, and which allow them to pass through immigration without a visa. Applications can be obtained from the Armenian Embassy in Washington, DC (Tel. 202-319-1976) or from the Consulate in Los Angeles, CA (Tel. 310-657-6102). The application fee is $350 if you apply in the US, and $300 if you apply in Armenia.

Special Residents, according to the Armenian Embassy, "enjoy the full protection of the law, as well as the rights and obligations of Armenian citizens." There are some notable exceptions. Special Residents may not vote or run for elected office, for example. They are also exempt from compulsory service in the armed forces. This residency passport is valid only for entry to Armenia, and cannot be used when arriving at any other country, including the country of your citizenship.

*Photograph: Woodlands at Lake Sevan, R. Kurkjian*

Karabagh does not issue its own passports, and offers no similar accommodation for ethnic Armenians who are citizens of other countries.

A simpler alternative is a one-year **temporary residency permit**, which is available to non-citizens who live and work full time in Armenia. The permit eliminates the need for an Armenian visa, but it cannot be used to gain access to other countries. Business travelers who intend to reside in Armenia for more than three months are required to obtain this residency permit from the Ministry of Internal Affairs after they arrive in Armenia. This permit will not grant the same travel privileges as exist for an Armenian citizen. Thus, you will still need a special visa if you wish to travel to Russia, even though Armenians do not. The permit is available from the Armenian Ministry of Internal Affairs, Passport and Visa Dept., located at 13a Mesrop Mashtots Ave. (Tel. 53-43-91).

## Registering with the US Embassy

The US Embassy does not require US citizens to register their presence, but if you are working full time in Armenia, registering will provide some perks. The embassy compound includes a movie theater, cafeteria, and a library, and if you are registered then you will be allowed to make an application for permission to use these facilities, for a modest annual fee. Because of the heightened security at all American government institutions worldwide, your name has to be on a list to do almost anything at the embassy. If you plan to be in country for several weeks or months, you might as well get on that list. To register, go to the consular office in Yerevan, the entrance to which is located on the left side of the Embassy building at 18 Baghramian Ave.

## Registering with the Armenian Authorities

It is illegal to operate a business in Armenia unless you have first registered with the State Register. More information is available from the State Department of Statistics, State Register and Analysis. The office is located near Republic Square, in the Third Government Building (Tel. 52-45-06; 52-46-00; Fax 52-10-21).

Journalists working in Armenia must register with the Foreign Ministry. There's no fee, and the form is not difficult to fill out. A letter of introduction from the journalist's employer is required. To register, journalists should bring their passport and two passport-sized photographs to the Ministry offices on Republic Square, where they will be issued press identification cards. Registration is also required in Karabagh. For details contact Karabagh's Representative to the US in Washington, DC (Tel. 202-347-5166).

## Advertising

If you plan to advertise your business, first check with the Ministry of Trade for relevant restrictions. According to the 1996 Advertising Law, Armenian is the official language of all advertising. This means that your advertisement must be produced primarily in Armenian, but text in a foreign language such as English is also allowed, provided the foreign text is smaller and subordinate to the Armenian. Advertisements in foreign language newspapers are exempt. There is also a prohibition on advertising certain goods, such as weaponry.

## Legal Counsel

Other regulations that affect business people are difficult to learn about. The regulations and laws are not always published in an accessible forum, and it is frequently difficult to obtain the information in English. Bureaucratic regulations can be complex and prone to frequent revision. For these reasons, it is advisable to consult with local lawyers about registration requirements and other business procedures. Information on lawyers can be obtained from the Consular section of the US Embassy. Information about lawyers from local sources is available from **Young Lawyers Union** (Tel. 58-17-71); **Lawyers Youth Organization** (Tel. 58-81-61); and **Advocates Collegia** (Tel. 58-34-42).

Essentials

## Investing

Armenia and the US are parties to a Bilateral Investment Treaty, commonly known as a BIT, which governs the conduct of investors. The treaty protects the property rights of US businesses in Armenia, and prohibits nationalization or confiscation. BIT also guarantees that US investors in Armenia will be treated the same as Armenian investors. In the parlance of the treaty, US investors are entitled to "national treatment." If there's a change in legislation in Armenia, foreign investors are entitled to elect to remain subject, for five years, to the laws that existed at the time the investment was made. The US does not recognize the independence of Karabagh, so there is of course no BIT between the two countries.

Foreigners have no right to own land, but they are allowed to own all other types of property. This prohibition on land ownership can be overcome by taking a long-term lease. A foreigner might also own land indirectly, by creating an Armenian business entity, which does have the right to own land. There is no prohibition on the ownership of improvements that are built upon the land, so foreigners may purchase apartments. The US Dept. of State has published a commercial guide that provides helpful information for business people. Their most recent publication is the *FY 2002 Country Commercial Guide: Armenia*, and it is available on their web site: www.state.gov. This guide is one of the sources for the information here on advertising, legal counsel and investments. The Armenian Development Agency (ADA) publication *Armenia Country Investment Profile 2000* includes recent data, but might be difficult to find in the US. To obtain a copy in Armenia, contact the ADA office in Yerevan (Tel. 57-01-70; Fax 54-22-72).

## Local Resources

For an alternative to costly professional translators and interpreters, you may wish to consider using a language student from one of Yerevan's universities. Briusov University, which is located at the corner of Tumanian and Sarian Streets in central Yerevan, can help you locate a student with an appropriate level of proficiency. Fees usually range from between one and five dollars per hour.

Conference facilities and temporary offices are available in Yerevan at a new **business center** operated by the American University of Armenia (AUA). The facility, known as the AUA Center, isn't as grand as a convention center, but its facilities include a 300-seat auditorium and state-of-the-art communications technology. It's located on Khanjian Street in central Yerevan. Further details are available from AUA headquarters, 300 Lakeside Drive, 4th Floor, Oakland, CA 94612 (Tel. 510-987-9452; Fax 510-208-3576) or directly from the facility in Yerevan (Tel. 15-10-48) (E-mail: mmkrtchi@aua.am).

For the closest thing to a **Yellow Pages**, purchase a copy of the annual directory that is published by **Spyur Co**. It's smaller than the phone books you may be accustomed to in the US, but this is the best source in the English language for businesses and organizations. Buy it for roughly $12 from the publisher at 1/3 Pavstos Buzandi Street, Yerevan (Tel. 59-00-00), or look at the online version (Internet: www.spyur.am). Other places to look for it in Yerevan: **Noyan Tapan** bookstore at Republic Square; **Avasa** Books at 25 Abovian Street.

For the Tbilisi (Georgia) Yellow Pages, which sells for about $18, contact Aradani Publishing (E-mail: aradani@kheta.ge) (Internet: www.aradani.kheta.ge). Karabagh does not have an English-language telephone directory.

*R. Kurkjian*                                                                 *Amberd Fortress*

# PHOTOGRAPHY

## HOW TO GET GREAT TRAVEL PHOTOS

For many Westerners, Armenia is an exotic and unknown place. Photography gives you an opportunity to put a face on this land, and to make Armenia real for friends and family who might otherwise never see it. Here are some suggestions that will help you to make the best of your travel photographs.

### Subject Matter

Armenia and Karabagh offer fantastic opportunities for **portrait and nature** photography. Most people in the villages and towns are thrilled to pose for photos. In Yerevan, which has a population of about one million, the people tend to get less excited. Still, we've found that a direct approach yields great results. If you want to take someone's picture, ask for permission. Almost everyone that we have ever asked has been flattered and has gotten a great kick out of trying to figure out why someone would want to take a picture of a total stranger! We've met some wonderful people this way, and made some good photographs, too. We are often asked for a copy of the photograph, but mail delivery to Armenia is notoriously poor, so we've had to improvise: we carry a Polaroid ® camera and we give them their gift on the spot.

There are generally no signs but **photography is prohibited** in the subway, at military installations, and outdoors at the airport. If you are apprehended, your film may be confiscated. But these places cannot compete with the marvelous subjects that are available throughout the countryside.

### Technique

When taking portraits, focus on the eyes, and avoid harsh and direct sunlight so that you won't end up with a portrait of someone squinting. Pay attention to the background, too. If there's a piece of trash at the person's foot, move it out of the photo. For a more flattering portrait, use a lens with a focal length of between 80-110mm. For the best portraiture, you will need to overcome any shyness you may have about photographing strangers. Talk to your subjects, gain their confidence, put them at ease, and your image will be improved.

For landscapes, you must use a tripod to get images with great clarity. This is because landscapes usually look best when the entire picture is in focus. In order to get the large depth of field that makes this possible, you have to close the aperture of the lens as much as possible. When you do this, you have to slow down the shutter speed, in order to get a correct exposure. And the only way to keep a camera absolutely still  is by mounting it on a tripod. For the greatest visual interest, include a focal point in the foreground, as well as in the background. This is particularly important if you are using a wide-angle lens, 35mm or wider.

## Composition

It is not necessary for everything in your photograph to be perfectly symmetrical. A person's face does not need to be dead center in the image. Place the face higher in the frame, and the image will be more pleasing to view. When photographing landscapes, don't try to include equal portions of sky and land. Instead, try framing the image so that only one third is occupied by sky. Or, if the skyscape is dramatic, try devoting only one third of the frame to the land. This is not a firm rule, but the composition will often be more dynamic if you arrange the frame in thirds, and if you avoid symmetrical compositions.

## Lighting

Lighting is an essential part of great photographs. In early morning, and just before sunset, the low position of the sun in the sky renders softer and richer colors. The intensity of the mid-day sun on a clear day will produce a harsh and unappealing white light which allows less detail than soft light. Open your eyes and really pay attention to your surroundings. Dramatic color changes occur throughout the day, and many of us don't even notice.

Bring an electronic flash. Outdoors, a flash can be used to fill in the shadows that might otherwise appear on a person's face, and to give a balanced look to a photograph that has a strong foreground, as well as a background that you want to emphasize. One example: a portrait of a person standing with Mt. Ararat in the background will often have a better exposure if you use a fill flash for the subject's face, even in daylight.

## What to Bring
### Cameras and Accessories

The photographic equipment that you use depends on the type of photographs you wish to take. If you only intend to record your trip, then a fully automatic (point-and-shoot) camera will suffice. However, if you want more flexibility and control, you will want, at a minimum, a camera system with interchangeable lenses, a flash unit, and a tripod. There are many camera formats to choose from and each has its advantages. The most popular format is a 35mm Single Lens Reflex (SLR). These are reasonably priced and relatively compact. A very useful lens is 35mm-85mm zoom lens. You may also want to bring a wide-angle lens, such as a 28mm for shooting landscapes, or a longer telephoto lens, of 200mm or more, for shooting portraits and capturing wildlife. This equipment will give you the ability to experiment with your technique (e.g., changing the depth of field) and provide you with the tools to make unique and interesting photographs.

There are numerous accessories one can use in photography. We recommend that you keep your equipment simple and become familiar with it so that you don't fumble with instruction manuals when in the field. Don't bring along extra gadgets that are a burden to lug around. Before your trip, make sure all your equipment is functioning properly. While traveling, keep it protected in a padded bag that you can comfortably carry with you.

*Photograph: At the central market in Stepanakert, R. Kurkjian*

Essentials

## Batteries

Special camera batteries are sometimes difficult to find, so bring extras with you. Size AA batteries, imported from Russia, are widely available, but their quality is suspect. Western brands such as Duracell and Eveready are available in Yerevan, but are difficult to locate outside the city. Batteries drain quickly in cold weather, sometimes after shooting only two rolls of film, so plan accordingly for winter visits and bring more than you think you will need.

## Filters and Cleaners

Keep a UV or Skylight filter on your lens to protect the lens surface from fingerprints, dirt, and permanent damage. Polarizers will help to reduce reflections and glare, such as the glare of the sun on a lake. A polarizer will also deepen the color of the sky so that it appears more natural in your image.

Yerevan and much of Armenia can get dry and dusty in the summer, making it difficult for you to keep your equipment clean. Bring a camel hair brush and air bulb to remove dust. Lens-cleaning fluid and lens tissue are also essential. Karabagh can frequently be rainy. Bring a waterproof camera bag to help keep your equipment dry.

## Film

The film you use is an important consideration that can have a dramatic effect on your image. What you intend to do with your photographs will dictate which film to use. Do you want to give a slide show, or place your prints in a photo album? There are artistic, practical and technical reasons for using color print, color slide, or black and white film. For instance, if you wish to enlarge your landscape photos and get brilliant color saturation, you should use a slow, fine-grain film (50 ISO). If you want to accurately reproduce skin tones, there is special film for this too. Typically, color print film has a wider latitude of exposure which means incorrect exposures can easily be corrected when printing. This is a better choice for point-and-shoot cameras. Slide film, on the other hand, has less room for error in exposure, but tends to produce more accurate color. You should first decide what type of photographs you want take, and then choose your film accordingly.

Regardless of which film you choose, bring it from home. You will be able to find plenty of color print film for sale in Yerevan and Stepanakert, but outside these cities film is difficult to locate. Be sure to check expiration dates and avoid film that has been exposed to the heat and sun, both of which will harm color reproduction.

## How to Store Film

Travelers need to give extra thought to safe film storage and handling. Before you leave home, remove the cans of film from their packaging, boxes and plastic containers. Place all of your film in a clear Ziploc® bag. The film is easier to carry around this way, and when you're ready to use a roll, you won't have to fumble with all that packaging. Bring an extra bag and use it for the film that you have exposed, so that you can keep those rolls separated from the unused film. Store the exposed film someplace cool and dark, until you can get it home for processing. A refrigerator is fine, as long as condensation doesn't form on the film canisters. Use a black permanent pen to identify the film canisters by date, place or event.

When you're touring, you'll want to bring extra film with you. Be careful not to leave the film in a hot car, or in direct sun, while you are out seeing the sights. A black camera bag can heat up quickly, as well, so use caution with the film you pack there.

## Airport Hazards

X-rays can ruin film, too. Absolutely never pack any film in the luggage that you check. Checked bags get subjected to high doses of x-rays, and your film will be damaged. Don't mail the film home, either, for the same reason. Instead, all of your film should be in your carry-on luggage when you travel by air.

Film with ISO ratings of 800 or higher can be damaged by the low-dosage x-rays that are used to scan luggage at the passenger gates, so always ask for a hand inspection of any high speed film that you carry onboard. Remove all the packaging from your film and carry it in a clear Ziploc® bag to facilitate the inspection. As an alternative to a hand inspection, place your film in a lead-lined film bag. These bags are designed for traveling with film, and you can purchase one at a camera shop. This lead won't stop the x-rays that are used for checked luggage, but it will protect film from the low-dose x-rays at the passenger gate.

*Essentials*

*Spandarian Reservoir in southern Armenia*                    R. Kurkjian

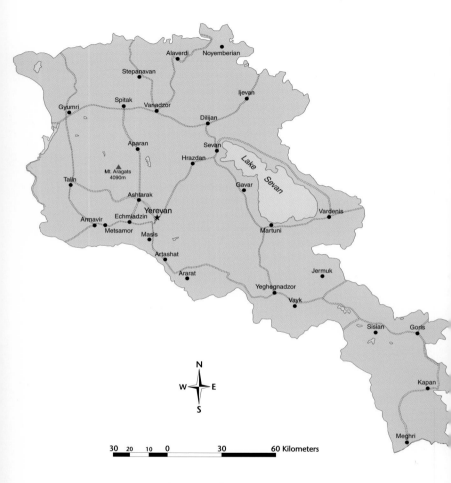

Armenia

# The Land and People

*Here, green and round, Armenia extends to three seas. Here, to two.
Here, to one. And here—not even to one. So swiftly does Armenia dimin-
ish from the first map to the last, always remaining a generally round
state, that if you riffle quickly through the atlas, it's a movie: it captures
the fall of a huge round stone from the altitude of millennia. The stone
disappears into the deep, diminishing to a point. But if you riffle the
pages from the end to the beginning, it's as if a small pebble has fallen
into the water, and historical circles are spreading across the water, ever
wider and wider.*

**–Andrei Bitov, *A Captive of the Caucasus***

Armenia was one of the major tourist destinations of the Soviet Union throughout the 1970s and 1980s. Travelers were directed here by the state-controlled
tourist agency, Intourist, and Intourist knew that it could rely upon Armenia to
show itself well.

This was the tiniest of the Soviet republics, all but lost in the shadow cast by Russia.
But it was also a showcase for cultural pride and national success. The standard of
living was high. The people were educated. Illiteracy was almost unheard of.

By the 1990s, however, independence and social upheaval had forced Armenia to
ignore tourism. And the tourists ignored Armenia. During the previous 3,000
years, Armenia had been overrun countless times by a litany of invaders, but the
people persevered, and they always rebuilt. During the 1990s, Armenians found
themselves rebuilding once again.

Today, Armenia is inviting the tourists to return and private enterprise has taken
over the tourist industry. Investors have built hundreds of new hotel rooms in
Yerevan, the capital city, and they have opened dozens of restaurants and shops. A
resurgence of tourism has begun. The number of foreign tourists traveling to
Armenia in 2001 surged to more than 123,000—an increase of 45 percent above
the previous year's tally—according to Armenia's National Statistical Service. More
than half of them were from the US and Europe.

This is a land of magnificent mountains and vistas. This is a country where you
can still get a cup of coffee for less than 20 cents, and where you can still get
invited to dinner each time you visit a different village. This is a country where
you won't find all the comforts of home, but where you may instead find something more important.

# GEOGRAPHY

Armenia is today located in southwestern Asia, east of Turkey. Its total area is 29,793 square kilometers, which is roughly the size of Belgium, or the US state of Maryland. The country is landlocked, and there are no navigable waterways. There are several fast-flowing rivers, however, and they are a significant source of electricity.

The country is mountainous, and has an average elevation of 1,800 meters above sea level. Only about 10 percent of the country lies below 1,000 meters. Forty percent lies at least 2,000 meters above sea level. The tallest mountain of historic Armenia is Mt. Ararat, which the Armenians call Masis. The taller peak, Mets (Big) Masis, reaches 5,165 meters. The smaller, and conical peak, Pokr (Little) Masis, is 3,925 meters. Ararat dominates the skyline of Yerevan, as well as much of the region around the Armenian capital. But this mountain is actually located in modern Turkey, just across the border. Inside modern Armenia, the tallest peak belongs to Mt. Aragats, which rises to 4,090 meters.

Forested lands are not common, and can be found mostly in the northern region surrounding Dilijan. Only approximately 12 percent of the country is either forest or woodland and there are no natural woodlands in the Yerevan area. Approximately 10 percent of the land is arable, and less than four percent is devoted to agriculture.

Lake Sevan, one of the largest alpine lakes in the world, is Armenia's largest water resource. Five percent of the surface area of Armenia is covered by this lake, and roughly 20 percent of the country lies within the vast Sevan watershed. The health of the lake is in great peril, however. Beginning in the 1930s, the Soviet government embarked on a scheme to reduce the surface area of the lake as a means toward reducing evaporation and thus increasing the commercial availability of its water. The lake bottom could also be farmed, or so it was thought. Vast amounts of water were diverted for irrigation and for hydroelectric generation.

By 1960, the level of the lake had decreased 19 meters, and the water volume had been diminished by more than 40 percent. Fishing harvests declined. Eutrophication increased. The survival of the lake was threatened. Commercial needs continue to threaten Lake Sevan, but scientists are today studying how to restore the delicate balance of its ecology, and the condition of the lake is a matter of widespread national concern. No one expects that the lake can be restored to its pre-1930 level. But there is hope that conditions will slowly improve, and that Lake Sevan will remain one of Armenia's greatest treasures.

Significant deposits of copper, zinc and aluminum exist, and there are small gold deposits as well. Rocks and minerals are a valuable commercial resource. Tuff (a pink-hued stone) and marble quarries produce abundant building materials. Obsidian is also plentiful. Diamonds are also mined, and exported for cutting.

The Land and People

Seismic activity is common throughout the country, and the susceptibility of the region to earthquakes has influenced the ancient architectural design of the churches, many of which have withstood repeated quakes. A significant earthquake struck the northern regions on December 7, 1988. Armenia's second largest city, Gyumri, was devastated by the quake and Spitak, the town nearest the epicenter, was leveled. More than 25,000 people were killed in a few moments of terror.

## CLIMATE

Armenia has a highland continental climate, marked by dry, hot summers and cold winters. The mountainous terrain contributes to the formation of several microclimates. As a result, it is not unusual for the weather to be hot and sunny in the capital city of Yerevan, while it is cold and rainy 55 km away at Lake Sevan.

Average temperatures in Yerevan and the Ararat Valley are –5 to +5 °C (25 to 40 °F) in winter. The absolute low is about -30 °C (–22 degrees F). Summer temperatures average 25 to 27 °C (75 to 80 °F) and top out at no more than 42 °C (106 °F). In the Lake Sevan region, winter temperatures range from –12 to +8 °C (10 F to 28 F), and summer temperatures are a more moderate 18 to 20 °C (65 to 70 °F). Current weather conditions for Armenia are available on the internet. Try: **www.wunderground.com** for both current and historical reports.

The most comfortable times to visit are during September and October. April and May can sometimes be rainy, but are otherwise fine times to travel. The intense sun and soaring temperatures of August, however, can be unpleasant.

**The Land and People**

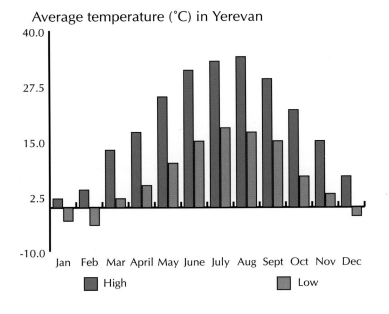

Average temperature (°C) in Yerevan

M. Karanian                                                    Vardavar

By tradition, Armenian children dump buckets of water on passersby on a set day, or two or three, in late July or early August. This is done in observance of a holiday known as **Vardavar**. The origins of this tradition are murky, but one rule is clear: children may do this with impunity. There's no indignity in being doused with water, but plenty of shame if you complain about it. Pleading to be spared is not unheard of, but we've even seen soldiers who prefer to simply accept the soaking rather than make a fuss. The dry weather, unrelenting sun, and temperatures that approach 38 °C (100 °F), may be the reason for the tolerance.

## CLOTHING

Lightweight clothes, made from natural fabrics, are best during Armenia's hot and dry summers. Hats and sunscreen are also advisable, to protect against the intense sun. Yerevan's semi-arid climate can make it dusty in the summer, so bring clothing that can be easily cleaned, or which will not show dirt.

Armenians take pride in the way they dress, and their attire is generally conservative. Short pants and tank tops are rarely worn in Armenia, except by young children, even on the hottest days. Men wear long pants. Older men frequently wear suits or sport coats. Women wear dresses or skirts. Dark colors are common.

If you are traveling in winter, be aware that most apartments and offices do not have central heating. Long underwear and woolen garments are advisable for use indoors as well as outside. Dressing in layers is the best way to trap your body's heat. Most body heat is lost through the top of the head, so be sure to wear a hat. Men will have to bring hats from home. We have found that stores rarely sell hats and gloves in men's sizes.

# POPULATION

Armenia's population is slightly more than 3 million according to the republic's most recent official census, which was conducted in 2001. This preliminary figure was released in 2002 and the government expects to have final results in 2003. This is Armenia's first census as an independent state. A tally conducted in 1989 during Soviet rule had revealed a population of 3.7 million. The decline is attributed to emigration, which has been caused by poor economic conditions.

Official government statistics from Karabagh in 2002 reveal a population of 144,000, of whom more than one-third lived in the capital city of Stepanakert. Both Karabagh and Armenia have ethnically homogenous populations. Ninety-six percent of Armenia's population is ethnic Armenian, and 90 percent of them are members, at least nominally, of the Armenian Apostolic Church. Kurds account for about two percent, and the balance is comprised of Russians, Greeks, Jews and expatriates from the West.

# LANGUAGE

*These are people who jangle the keys of their language even when they are not using them to unlock any treasures.*

**–Osip Mandelstam**

Armenian is the official language of Armenia, and it is spoken and written by nearly everyone. Russian is widely spoken, and many in the older generation prefer it to Armenian. The Armenians call themselves Hye, and they call their country Hayastan. The name is a derivative of the legendary Haik, a lineal descendant of Noah, to whom the Armenians trace their ancestry.

Among the younger generation, Armenian is the primary tongue, and English is widely studied. As a result, it is easy to find a young person in Yerevan who can translate from Armenian to English. Students at the Briusov University at the corner of Tumanian and Sarian Streets, and at the American University of Armenia on Baghramian Ave., can be helpful with interpretation services of varying proficiencies, for fees of between one and five dollars per hour. If you make arrangements in advance, you should not have difficulty finding students who are willing to travel outside Yerevan for several hours of work. Professionals are also available, at considerably higher fees.

Most business signs in Yerevan are in both Armenian and English, and English is usually spoken by at least one worker at the larger offices and stores. Foreigners who attempt to speak Armenian are warmly received and generally encouraged to continue.

Two major types of Armenian are widely used today. Eastern Armenian is spoken in the Republic of Armenia and among the Armenians of Iran. Western Armenian was prevalent in the western Armenian provinces until 1915, and is today still spoken by many Armenians in the Diaspora. There are other regional dialects spoken throughout Armenia and Karabagh. The Armenian Church uses an ancient form of the language for its liturgy.

## ECONOMY

Armenia entered a period of economic decline beginning in 1988, when a massive and devastating earthquake struck its northwestern region, including Gyumri, then known as Leninakan, the country's second-largest city. The economy was stabilized and inflation was brought under control by 1995, however, and the country is today struggling to develop a free-market system. These efforts have been discouraged by Armenia's neighbors, Turkey and Azerbaijan, which have both blockaded Armenia for the past decade. As a result, supply routes are circuitous, and trade is hampered.

There is an abundant supply of electricity, however, thanks to a combination of thermal, hydroelectric, and nuclear power. Indeed, there is a surplus at times, which is sold to electricity-starved Georgia. Armenia's nuclear plant, which went online in 1980, is nearing the end of its lifespan. The president, Robert Kocharian, has pledged to close the plant by 2004, but only if alternative energy sources are located. Alternatives are unlikely as long as its neighbors blockade the country, however. And so, with international assistance, the Armenian government has instead spent millions of dollars on upgrades and safety precautions at the nuclear power plant. International observers report that the plant, which does not have a Chernobyl-style design, is safe.

Ample supplies of electricity have not resulted in significant economic growth. The per capita GDP is roughly $490, and the total GDP is about $1.9 billion, according to recent figures released by the World Bank. The total GDP is projected to increase at a rate of 5.6 percent each year through 2003. Major natural resources are copper, zinc and gold. The primary agricultural products are fruits and vegetables, wines, and some livestock.

Jewelry and precious stones account for 34 percent of Armenia's exports. Minerals and metals account for an additional 24 percent. Roughly one third of the country's imports are foodstuffs. The country's largest trading partners are Russia (24 percent), Turkmenistan (20 percent), Iran (13 percent) and Georgia (seven percent). Trade with countries of the European Union accounts for another 15 percent. The World Bank projects that exports will increase at the rate of about 11 percent each year through 2003.

Fifty-five percent of those who have jobs in the private sector are employed in agriculture. Twenty-five percent work in the services sector, and 20 percent are employed in manufacturing, mining and construction. Forty-five percent of the population lives below the poverty line.

For additional information try www.state.gov, operated by the US Dept. of State, and www.odci.gov/cia/publications/factbook/geos/am/html, operated by the Central Intelligence Agency. The World Bank and the United States Agency for International Development (USAID) are also good sources of information.

# POLITICS

## Framework

Armenia is a democratic republic. The government is hybrid in form, and consists of both an elected president and a prime minister who is selected by the president. The President is the chief of state. The Prime Minister is the head of government. The cabinet is formed by a council of ministers that is appointed by the prime minister.

The legislature consists of a unicameral parliament, which is known as the National Assembly. Its 131 members represent several political parties, ranging from Republicans to Communists. The nation's judicial branch consists of both a Supreme Court and a special Constitutional Court that is empowered to hear only cases of constitutional significance.

Armenia's constitution was adopted by referendum in 1995, and it is a document of great aspiration. Extraordinary constitutional guarantees include housing, medical care, and education, but the government lacks the money to implement them. Other guarantees, such as the right to travel, are reminders of past repression while under Soviet rule. There is universal suffrage for all citizens who have reached the age of 18 years. In addition to being a document of high aspirations, it is also a document of strong presidential power. Several changes and amendments were proposed in 2001 in an effort to limit the president's authority, and to increase citizen access to the courts. The proposals were prompted by Armenia's recent membership in the Council of Europe, and many observers considered it likely that the proposals would eventually lead to another nationwide referendum on the constitution.

The legal system is based upon civil law, which is dramatically different from the common law system in the US and the UK. There are no juries, but it is common for a case to be heard by three judges, each of whom takes such an active role in the proceedings that the private lawyers sometimes appear to be superfluous. Cases are decided not by legal precedent, but instead by reference to the code of laws. This legal system is common in continental Europe.

## Leadership

President Robert Kocharian assumed the office of president on February 3, 1998, upon the resignation of the country's first elected president, Levon Ter Petrosian. Kocharian was elected in a special election the following month. The president appointed Andranik Margarian to the position of Prime Minister on May 12, 2000.

The Land and People

# ECOLOGY

By Daniel Klem, Jr.

Although relatively small in size, Armenia is rich, extravagantly rich, in natural history. Its mix of varying soils, climatic conditions, elevations, waters, and other resources supports a diverse assemblage of living species. All life is important to a healthy Armenia, but select groups and even specific species have been and continue to be historically attractive to Armenians, and to those who visit this unique and special country. Increasingly, visitors are traveling to Armenia specifically to see its natural beauty and wildlife.

## Natural Habitats

With the exception of tropical rain forests, all of the world's eight major biological communities are represented in Armenia. From these communities or from their subdivisions, there are five prominent natural habitats in the republic: semi-desert, mountain steppe, forest, mountain meadow, and water. They each have unique elements that make them easily identifiable as you move about the country.

**Semi-desert** predominates in southern Armenia, and is characterized by a cover of sage plants and rock. It is dry and typically below 1,000 meters with unique floral assemblages. **Mountain steppe** is also dry land at altitudes between 1,200 to 2,000 meters consisting of grasses interspersed with rocky outcrops and shrubs of varying heights. **Forests** occur in various sized patches at elevations between 550 to 2,600 meters and are composed mainly of deciduous beech, oak, and hornbeam trees. Few cone-bearing trees such as pine are present. **Mountain meadow** is found at higher elevations between 2,200 to 4,090 meters and consists of a variety of cover types that include grasses, shrubs, bare soil, rocks, and snow. Although **water** is moderately represented in the overall area within the republic, many Armenian wetlands have been drained or debilitated for hydroelectric power, the irrigation of crops, and to expose additional land for the development of human settlements or increased croplands. Wetlands in general are nutrient rich, they provide breeding grounds for waterfowl and other wildlife, and they filter and store water. They are extremely valuable wildlife habitats, and responsible management can help prevent their loss.

## Flora and Fauna

The varied landscape of Armenia currently hosts an overall biological diversity that merits protection to ensure local and regional environmental health and to maintain its living treasures. There are approximately 3,200 plants forming many unique and varied combinations covering the land. Like elsewhere on Earth, uncountable numbers of species and individuals of invisible microbes and often-invisible invertebrates such as bacteria and insects populate all habitat types. These are the principal decomposers, cleaners, and food sources of the more visible and familiar vertebrate animals such as fish, amphibians, reptiles, birds, and mammals. More than 500 different species of vertebrates occur within the borders of Armenia.

Armenia's charismatic large mammals and all of its birds are especially sensitive indicators of environmental health. Bears, boar, leopard, wolf, ibex, and mouflon are intriguing and of intense interest. Because of their exceptionally wild and secretive life styles, these animals can be found only with great effort and typically only within the republic's designated and protected reserves and reservations.

*Photograph: Mt. Aragats, M. Karanian*

# Reserves, Reservations and National Parks

The government of Armenia recognizes the need to conserve its natural areas, and has designated roughly ten percent of the country as protected areas. Since 1958 it has established five reserves, numerous reservations, and a national park, in an effort to protect the country's unique flora, fauna, and natural areas. The reserves are given protected status, and human activity, officially at least, is limited to scientific research.

In the **Khosrov Reserve**, which is perhaps the country's most famous, a convergence of the Mediterranean, Georgian and Iranian floristic zones contributes to the region's great diversity of flora. More than 1,800 of Armenia's 3,200 plant species are native to the reserve's 70,000 acres. The rare Anatolian leopard is also a native, and may have been one of the animals that were hunted on this land by the reserve's namesake, King Khosrov II, during his fourth century AD reign.

Armenia's greatest natural treasure, however, is Lake Sevan, its only national park. This is the second largest alpine inland body of freshwater in the world, second only to Lake Geneva in Switzerland. Sevan and its surrounding adjacent wetlands are the major attraction for both resident and migratory water birds in the southern Caucasus region.

**The Land and People**

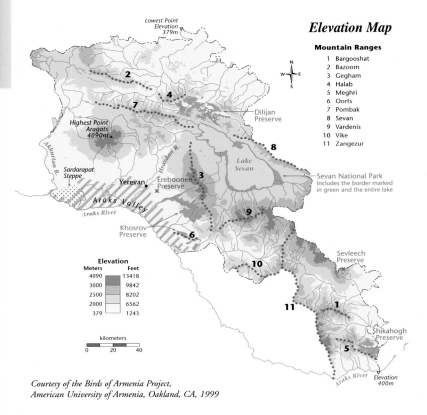

*Courtesy of the Birds of Armenia Project,*
*American University of Armenia, Oakland, CA, 1999*

# Birds

Armenia's birds highlight the nation's living diversity and rich natural beauty. Approximately two-thirds of the birds known to exist in all of Europe can be found within this country, where one can reasonably expect to be able to visit all of its varying habitats. Dominic Mitchell, the publisher and editor of Britain's best selling birding magazine, reports that Armenia is "surely the region's next big birding hot-spot."

EURASIAN HOOPOE

About one-third of Europe's species of special concern—those that are identified as declining, endangered or threatened—are present and often prominent in Armenia. Just a few of these prized birds are the Armenian Gull, Radde's Accentor, Finsch's Wheatear, the Ortolan and Grey-necked Buntings, and the Red-fronted Serin. Other birds that are more challenging to find and that are highly sought after are the White-tailed Lapwing, the Caspian Snowcock, and the Caucasian Black Grouse.

Armenia has been a crossroads of the world not just for humans, but also for all forms of wildlife. Few animals exemplify this migration more dramatically than birds of prey. Birders call these animals raptors, and they are the spectacular eagles, hawks, falcons, and harriers that are found in Armenia. Many of their kind live here year-round, but many more pass through

CAUCASIAN GROUSE Armenia on their seasonal movements south each fall and north each spring. They thereby escape the harsh northern winters but return to breed among the rich resources of a new growing season. The sheer number of these attractive and powerful birds offers further evidence of the wealth of animal diversity in these lands. Over a year's time, tiny Armenia hosts 35 separate species, which is roughly the same number that would be found over all of North America.

Of the approximately 550 species of birds present in all of Europe, 346 have been officially recorded in Armenia. This spectacular avian diversity within a modest geographic area makes Armenia an attractive destination for birders willing to travel the globe to find and identify the world's 10,000 species of birds.

The diverse habitat at varying elevations explains the attraction of the Armenian landscape for many different kinds of birds. The current species diversity and massive volume of the migratory passage of birds is attributed to countless populations moving from their breeding grounds to the northwest, north, and northeast regions of the Eurasian continent, to non-breeding grounds either within Armenia or to the south in the Middle East or Africa. Distribution maps in *A Field Guide to Birds of Armenia* highlight those areas where appropriate habitats for a species exist, but where the species has not been officially recorded. These maps invite observers to discover new locations for each species by searching the designated prospective areas.

CASPIAN SNOWCOCK

This beautiful land filled with unimaginably attractive wildlife invites you to visit. And, to whatever degree is appropriate, it beckons you to join in the development and implementation of conservation plans to ensure that all Armenia's natural resources will remain intact and available to current and future generations.

*Daniel Klem, Jr., Ph.D., D.Sc., is the co-author, along with Martin S. Adamian, Ph.D., of* A Field Guide to Birds of Armenia *(American University of Armenia, 1997).*

The Land and People

# TWO THOUSAND YEARS OF CHRISTIANITY

The Armenians consider themselves among the world's first Christians and they attribute their survival as a distinct people to their faith. Christianity united the nation during its long periods of foreign domination, and it enabled the Armenians to preserve their culture and national identity. As Christians in a part of the world that would become, and which still is, predominantly Muslim, the Armenians were able to avoid assimilation and maintain a cohesive society even without political independence.

The earliest Christians in Armenia had been converted in the first century AD by Christ's Apostles Thaddeus and Bartholomew. The missionary work of these Apostles eventually resulted in Armenia's official repudiation of paganism. In an acknowledgement of its ancient origins, the church of Armenia is called the Armenian Apostolic Church.

The nation officially adopted Christianity in AD 301 when a man named Gregory persuaded King Trdat that the king's realm should be Christian, and not pagan. The king, ironically, had imprisoned this man thirteen years earlier for the crime of preaching Christianity. Gregory had been sent to prison, actually a dungeon pit, for his supposed lunacy, and he is said to have survived only because other Christians had secretly brought him food and water.

The king didn't fare as well and had gone mad in the meantime. According to the legend, Gregory prayed for the king and cured him. And so the king expressed his gratitude by proclaiming Christianity as the official faith for the nation. Gregory was sainted, and he is now known as St. Gregory the Illuminator. The pit where he was imprisoned still exists, and a monastery was built above it as a demonstration of Christianity's triumph. Visitors can climb down into the pit, at the monastery of Khor Virap, in the town of Artashat. The monastery gates are open daily from 10 am until 5 pm, but visitors can still see plenty from outside the wall after hours.

Of course, Christianity in Armenia predates AD 301. And since the church traces its lineage directly to Christ, the Armenians might just as properly be celebrating their nation's 2,000-year-old Christian heritage. But the practice of

*Photographs:*
*Echmiadzin Cathedral (left), M. Karanian and new construction in Vayk (right), R. Kurkjian*

Christianity wasn't freely permitted until the king's decree, so Armenians logically settled upon 2001 as the year for commemorating the 1,700th anniversary of their faith. Special activities were held all year long to mark the date. The two biggest events were a visit by the Pope and the consecration of the new St. Gregory the Illuminator Cathedral in Yerevan.

Visitors who missed the opportunity to travel to Armenia for the 1,700th anniversary celebrations can still take advantage of many Holy site pilgrimages that are arranged by church authorities each year. For detailed information about events, the official church web site is helpful: www.etchmiadzin.com. Any questions about events can be sent by e-mail to 1700@etchmiadzin.com. Don't forget the letter 't' when typing these addresses.

Mail or telephone inquiries may be directed to the **Diocese of the Armenian Church**, 630 Second Ave., New York, NY 10016 (Tel. 212-686-9893; Fax 212-686-0245) or the **Prelacy of the Armenian Church**, 138 East 39th Street, New York, NY 10016 (Tel. 212-689-7810; Fax 212-689-7168).

*M. Karanian*                    *1700th anniversary of Christianity observation at Khor Virap Monastery*

*New Years Eve 2001, Yerevan*                                                                                      *R. Kurkjian*

*R. Kurkjian*

# THE ANCIENT ART OF CARPET WEAVING

By James Tufenkian

The art of carpet weaving in the land of Armenia is truly ancient. No one really knows for sure, but there is good reason to believe that the art originated there. In any case, it is clear that until about four hundred years ago Armenian carpet weaving was preeminent in the world, and was generally recognized as being so.

Marco Polo, the famous world traveler who must have seen many carpets, was one of the many admirers of Armenian carpets. In his thirteenth century account of travels through ancient Armenia, he observed that it was among the Greeks and Armenians "where the best and most beautiful carpets are produced, as well as silk of crimson and other splendid colors."

Perhaps we shouldn't be surprised by Polo's comments. There is evidence, after all, that carpet weaving in the area of ancient Armenia was already a refined art five centuries before the birth of Christ. In 1949 archeologists discovered the oldest intact carpet known today in a royal tomb hidden in the Altai Mountains of Mongolia. Amazingly, the Pazyryk Carpet, as it is called, is not the rough and primitive product of an early society. It is instead considered to be finely knotted and highly evolved, even by today's standards.

European scholars have argued convincingly that the origin of the Pazyryk Carpet was in pre-Armenian Urartu, based on its design elements which are documented in surviving Urartian monuments, and in its depiction of Hittite dress and horse ornaments. Analysis of the red dyes used in the carpet show that they originated in the Ararat plain where they were recognized for thousands of years as an exclusive product of the region.

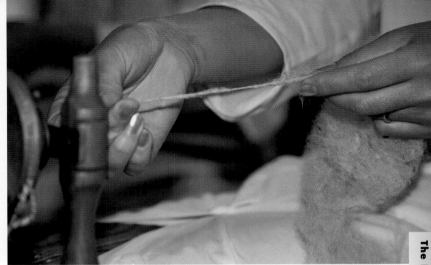

Armenian carpets were traded to the corners of the known world, but they reached their extraordinary level of development because they were an essential part of the fabric of Armenian life. Armenian sources refer to carpets being used to adorn the floors and walls of churches beginning in the fifth century, and describe sumptuous meals consumed while seated on these carpets.

Records, literature, and historical accounts from Greek, Roman, Persian, Arab, Bulgarian and other sources mention Armenian carpets given in tribute, paid as taxes, or taken as booty, beginning in pre-Christian times. Surprisingly, Arab sources acknowledge the supremacy of Christian Armenian prayer rugs, even though these rugs are often thought of as the quintessential Islamic art form. What is also remarkable from historical accounts is that the Armenian carpets were not merely the small products of home looms, but were the result of organized commercial enterprises that created huge works of exceptional beauty. A single carpet sometimes covered as much as 60 square meters.

All of this began to change, as did the association of Armenians with the weaving of great carpets, when the Armenian kingdom of Cilicia fell in AD 1375. At that time many Armenians fled their homeland and settled in Egypt, Transylvania, Poland, and Persia. Not coincidentally, it was during this time that carpet weaving became prominent among the Mamluks of Egypt and in the other regions where Armenians settled. They carried their craft with them and transferred it to the populations of their host countries.

At the beginning of the seventeenth century, the Persian Shah Abbas transplanted 100,000 Armenians from their homes in Julfa, which is in modern Nakhijevan, to New Julfa, constructed outside of the holy city of Isfahan in Persia. He gave them a monopoly on the silk trade, sending them to India where they created flourishing commercial outposts. It is from this time that the greatest carpets of Persia and

Moghul India were created. At the same time, the famous Polish court carpets known as Polonaise were woven in Isfahan, and presented to the royalty of Poland which, by then, had a thriving community of more than 100,000 Armenians.

Great carpet weaving followed the Armenians wherever they settled but, unfortunately, the Armenian contribution to weaving has been obscured. Armenians, a people without a country, came to be known as merely the traders who brought the carpets of their adoptive lands to the corners of the world. During the past several centuries, Armenians have been identified mainly with the great carpets of the Caucasus, despite their undeniable contribution in creating the much-admired Oushak carpets of Anatolia, and the Tabriz carpets of northwestern Iran.

Armenian carpets from the Caucasus are as magnificent as they are diverse. Early on, the bold Dragon carpets of the seventeenth century were created. Later, beginning in the early nineteenth century, came the French-influenced floral carpets that were made in Nagorno Karabagh for members of the Russian aristocracy. Prized by collectors for the past century, Armenian Caucasian carpets are characterized by their powerful and inspired designs, their brilliant colors, and their velvety wool pile.

During Soviet times the cottage industry of carpet weaving practiced by most Armenian women of the time was slowly strangled. Individual enterprise was discouraged, and the carpet industry was centralized into a monolithic state organization that monopolized the craft. Not surprisingly, Soviet values emphasized quantity and conformity over passion and creativity, which was devastating to the continuation of the lively folk art tradition of carpet weaving. Consequently, most of the Soviet-era carpets are as bland and uninspired as the workplaces in which they were created.

Fortunately, with the fall of the Soviet system and the independence of Armenia, there is now a movement underway to revive the artistry of ancient Armenian carpet making. Paramount are the old values—use of the best indigenous Caucasian mountain wool, yarn brushed and spun entirely by hand, and colors inspired by the great carpets of the past.

Once again, beautiful carpets with integrity and spirit are being created in Armenia, commanding high prices and great respect in the markets of Europe and North America. In the process, thousands of people are proudly employed in the revival of this truly Armenian art form.

*James Tufenkian is President of Tufenkian Carpets, which produces and exports more than 10,000 square feet of Armenian carpets each month.*

# A HISTORY OF ARMENIA

By Ronald Grigor Suny

For three thousand years historians and travelers have recorded the presence of a people called the Armenians in what is today eastern Turkey and the South Caucasus. The history of Armenia has been told as a tale of heroes and martyrs, of an ancient people who somehow survived the onslaughts of invasions, conquests, natural disasters, and near annihilation at the hands of imperial powers.

A central theme has been survival and endurance, a search for security and dignity. For many centuries these people maintained an identity—first pagan and later Christian—without a state of their own. Their national church provided the focus of unity, and its priests and monks perpetuated the literary and artistic traditions that marked the Armenians. In the twentieth century, after more than five hundred years without a state, Armenians set up an independent republic in the South Caucasus. That state was soon Sovietized, and for seven decades was part of the Soviet Union. At the dawn of the twenty-first century, Armenians are once again divided between those who live in the newly independent Republic of Armenia and those who are scattered around the world in the Diaspora.

Armenia historically was a mountainous land of more than 100,000 square miles with its ancient centers in the valley of the Arax River and the region around Lake Van in what is now the Republic of Turkey. Living on the Armenian plateau continuously from the seventh century BC until driven out of Turkish Armenia in 1915, most Armenians were peasant farmers who managed to cultivate the rugged land despite the bitterly cold winters and fiercely hot summers. Throughout their long history, threats from invaders and marauding nomads encouraged many Armenians to migrate to towns or to foreign countries and form new Armenian communities in the Middle East, Russia, Poland, Western Europe, India, and America. Today more Armenians live outside of the Armenian Republic than within. That tiny country of 11,000 square miles today faces hostile countries to the east and west, bears up under a crippled economy and an inconclusive struggle for the region of Karabagh, which had been part of the neighboring Soviet republic of Azerbaijan. The capital of the Armenian Republic, Yerevan, is the country's largest city, a modern city of more than a million inhabitants.

## The Earliest Times

Humans first settled on the Armenian plateau about six thousand years BC, and the first major state was the kingdom of Urartu, with its center around Lake Van. Excavated and restored monuments from the Urartian period can be found in Yerevan, which was founded by the Urartians as the citadel of Erebuni. Shortly after the fall of Urartu, the Indo-European-speaking proto-Armenians migrated, probably from the West, onto the Armenian plateau and mingled with the local peoples. The first mention of the Armenians dates from the mid-sixth century BC in an inscription at Behistun.

The Land and People

60

*National Geographic Maps/NGS Image Collection*

Culturally, Armenia stood between the world of ancient Persia and ancient Greece, its traditions a blend of Hellenism and Iranism. Ruled for many centuries by the Persians, Armenia became a buffer state between the Greeks and Romans to the West and the Persians or Arabs of the Middle East. It reached its greatest size under King Tigran II, the Great, (95-55 BC), who fought but ultimately succumbed to the Romans. Tigran, whose crowned head can be seen on coins of his era, built his capital at Tigranakert in southeastern Anatolia. A major monument in the Republic of Armenia, the temple at Garni, bears witness to the classical heritage in Armenia.

## Religion

A distinctly Armenian culture may be said to begin with the conversion to Christianity. Armenian tradition traces Armenian origins back to the handsome giant, Haik, the lover of independence, who killed the evil Bel, but these tales come down to us in early sources of the Christian era. Grandparents tell their grandchildren about the earliest Armenians, descendents of Noah, whose ark landed on Mount Ararat, or of the Armenian language spoken by all humanity before the Tower of Babel confused the tongues. And Armenians repeatedly tell their acquaintances, Armenian or *odar* (non-Armenian), that they were the first Christian state. Even before the official conversion of the Armenians, there were Christians in Armenia. This is attested to in the Armenian tradition of the antiquity of the Armenian Church, which was founded by apostles of Christ.

At the end of the third century AD, Armenia came under the protection of Rome once again. Parts of the eastern Roman empire, like Cappadocia, were already Christianized, and a priest from Caesarea named Gregory (Grigor) entered

Armenia to proselytize the faith. The Armenian king, Trdat III, was a protégé of the Roman emperor Diocletian, who persecuted the Christians in the empire. Trdat loathed the Christians as well and had Gregory tortured and thrown into a pit (Khor Virap). In the story told by the fifth century historian Agathangelos, Gregory remained in the pit for fifteen years.

Meanwhile, the king cruelly murdered Christian nuns, Hripsime and Gayane, who were escaping from Diocletian, and for his actions was turned into a wild boar. Trdat's sister dreamt that Gregory could save the king. The holy man preached to the king for sixty-five days after which Trdat agreed to accept Christianity and build a cathedral at Vagharshapat (Echmiadzin). Nearby he erected chapels to commemorate the martyred nuns. Saint Gregory the Illuminator became the first Catholicos of the new church.

Both theologically and politically the Armenians stood apart from the Orthodoxy of the Byzantine Empire to the west and the Mazdeist, and later Muslim, world of Persia to the east. Armenia was a buffer zone to be sure, but this also meant that it would be buffeted by more powerful states in their wars against one another.

In the first years of the next century Saint Mesrop, known as Mashtots, invented an alphabet so that the Gospel could be revealed to the Armenians. In the fifth century, considered the "Golden Age" of Armenian literature, important religious and historical works appeared that provided a foundation for a distinguished literary tradition. The Armenian historian Yeghishe tells the story of the struggle of Armenians under Prince Vardan Mamikonian against the attempt of the Persians to impose their religion on Armenia. At the battle of Avarair in AD 451, the Armenians fought to the death against the Persians to preserve their faith. That day, Vardanants, when hundreds of Armenians died in service of Christianity, is still marked as a major national holiday by Armenians, and Vardan is venerated as a saint. Later generations of writers turned the Armenian martyrs of the fifth century AD author Yeghishe, who were largely concerned about salvation and eternity, into patriotic defenders of the nation who loved the soil of their motherland, Armenia.

## The Middle Ages

Medieval Armenia was characterized by small kingdoms and princedoms. Faced by powerful enemies in the East, like the Persians, and in the West, by Rome and later Byzantium, the Armenians seldom united under a single monarch. Very often the various noble houses of Armenia fought with one another and with their kings. Indeed, in AD 428 the nobles petitioned the Persian king to eliminate the monarchy in Armenia.

Some analysts argue, however, that it was precisely the diversity of the Armenian principalities that helped preserve Armenia. Instead of a single kingdom that could have been conquered by invaders seizing the capital and subduing the king, Armenia presented its enemies with many semi-independent polities that had to be overrun one by one.

This powerful system of autonomous princes, or *nakharars*, marked the social structure of Armenia from antiquity until the Mongol invasions of the thirteenth century. Seventy or eighty important families, like the Mamikonians, the Bagratunis, and the Artsrunis, commanded thousands of armed warriors, lived off landed estates, and governed their realms from fortified castles. The *nakharars* held their land in hereditary tenure, though occasionally a king might have seized the land for some reason. In Armenia these aristocrats were as powerful, sometimes more powerful, than the person designated king.

Armenian medieval civilization was faced by two great threats in the seventh century. From the west, the expanding Byzantine Empire moved against the Persians and attempted to integrate Armenians back into the Orthodox religious world. From the south, the Arabs, newly converted to Islam, moved through the Middle East into Armenia and the South Caucasus. Armenians used the competing imperialisms to maneuver a degree of autonomy in the face of these dual dangers. The Armenian princes estimated that the Arabs were the lesser danger and did not resist the Arab invasions very vigorously at first. In the words of Sepeos the Bishop, the *nakharars* "made an accord with death and an alliance with Hell."

Armenians actually thrived after the initial Arab conquest of Greater Armenia, but later Arab rulers proved to be far more brutal than their predecessors. In the eighth century, Armenians revolted against the Arabs, and the Muslims crushed the rebellions and turned their rage against the Armenian princes. Yet one Armenian princely family, the Bagratunis, benefited from their alliance with the Arabs and soon emerged as the new kings of Armenia and Georgia. The repeated invasions of the Byzantines and Arabs brought chaos and destruction to Armenia. In 855 the Caliph sent an enormous army that killed 30,000 Armenians. Whole areas of the country were de-Armenized and settled by Muslims. Arab emirates co-existed with small Armenian principalities and the kingdoms of the Bagratunis. Where Armenians were able to keep control and maintain a degree of internal security, they continued building their churches, writing their histories, and illustrating their manuscripts. The eighth to the eleventh centuries were simultaneously a period of high culture amid great danger.

In the tenth century the Byzantine Empire annexed parts of historic Armenia, even as the Bagratuni kingdoms reached their zenith. King Gagik I "the Great" expanded his kingdom and crowned it by building the Cathedral at Ani, now lying across the border in Turkey. Almost all of western Armenia came under Byzantine control by the early eleventh century. Armenia was no longer a serious buffer for the Byzantines when suddenly from the east came the first Turkish invaders, the Seljuks. In the 1030s the Seljuks entered Armenia, and in 1064 they took the Bagratuni capital, Ani. The Armenian chronicler, Aristakes Lastivertsi, lamented: "The number of people massacred and the incalculable number of corpses turned the great river that flows near the city red with blood. The dead found their graves in the stomachs of savage beasts and domesticated animals, for no one was able to bury them or spread dirt on their bodies." In 1071 the Seljuks defeated the

Byzantine army at Manzikert and captured the emperor, initiating the long, slow decline of the Byzantine Empire.

One by one, the independent Armenian kingdoms in Greater Armenia collapsed. Thousands of Armenians fled south to the Mediterranean coast where several princes established small states that eventually formed the princedom, later kingdom, of Cilician Armenia. The Armenian kingdom received the Crusaders from Western Europe and fought against the rising Muslim threat to Christendom until it was overrun by Mamluks in 1375. Cilician Armenia's greatest moments came in the reign of Levon II "the Magnificent" (1187-1219). As ruler of one of the most important states in the Middle East, the king joined with Richard the Lionhearted in the conquest of Cyprus. The tiny kingdom imitated the feudal political forms of the Western Europeans and engaged in vigorous trade with Genoa and Venice. The Armenian Church drew close to the Roman Catholic Church for a time, as European influence flooded over the Armenian kingdom. The last kings of Armenia were, in fact, more French than Armenian. Overwhelmed by superior forces, the last king of Armenia, Levon VI, was taken captive by the Mamluks to Egypt. Later ransomed by the king of Castile, Levon died in Paris and was buried with the kings of France in the church at St. Denis outside of Paris.

After several centuries of devastation and despair at the hands of Turks and Mongols, Greater Armenia was once again divided between the Ottoman Turks and the Persians. Population in Armenia fell; towns shrank in size; and much of Armenia reverted to agriculture. From the fifteenth century until the early twentieth century, most Armenians lived in the Ottoman Empire, while a smaller number in eastern Armenia were ruled by the Persians. A few surviving Armenian nobles maintained some political power in the small melikdoms of Karabagh, Sisian, Kapan, and Lori.

## The Modern Era

The nineteenth century has been called the "Age of Nationalism." The idea that humanity is naturally divided into nations and that these nations should have the right to govern themselves became a powerful source of political mobilization in the decades after the French Revolution of 1789-1799. Already in the eighteenth and early nineteenth centuries, Armenian scholars wrote patriotic histories, poems, and plays extolling the notion that an ancient Christian people was unjustly suffering under the Muslim yoke.

In the late nineteenth century, as the Ottoman Empire declined, Armenians in Turkey complained of arbitrary taxation, seizures of property, and the periodic attacks of armed Kurds. Russia and Britain took an interest in their plight, and after the Russo-Turkish War of 1877-1878, the victorious Russians forced the Turkish sultan to agree to reforms in the Armenian provinces of eastern Anatolia. But at the Congress of Berlin in 1878, the Great Powers of Europe forced the Russians to back down and left the Armenians with few gains. Although much talk revolved around the so-called "Armenian Question," no real reforms were carried out to protect the

Armenians from their Muslim rulers. Frustrated and angry, young Armenians turned from working within the Ottoman system to organizing small revolutionary parties. The Turkish authorities responded brutally to what they perceived to be an Armenian threat to the stability of the empire. The "Bloody Sultan" Abdul Hamid II armed Kurdish irregulars and sanctioned the massacre of hundreds of thousands of Armenians in 1894-1896.

## Genocide and Wrongful Denial

When World War I broke out and Turkey went to war with Russia, Armenians found themselves on both sides of the front. In a fierce campaign in the winter of 1914-1915, the Russian army, aided by Armenian volunteers from Russia, dealt a severe blow to the Ottoman forces. The Young Turk leaders, fueled by the accumulated hatreds and suspicions of the Armenians, decided to deport Armenians from their historic homeland into the deserts of Mesopotamia. Orders went out to demobilize the Armenian soldiers serving in the Ottoman Army, and they soon were murdered. Then the authorities turned on civilians, women and children, forcing them out of their homes and marching them through mountains and valleys toward Syria. In the process, hundreds of thousands of Armenians, perhaps as many as a million and a half, died or were massacred in what most historians call the first genocide of the twentieth century. International opinion at the time condemned the "holocaust" launched by the Turks against their Armenian subjects, but in time the events of 1915 were slowly forgotten – though not by Armenians.

Decades later, the Turkish government organized and financed an official campaign to deny that the Ottoman state was responsible for the killings of the Armenians or that the massacres constituted a genocide. Rather the deaths and deportations, they claimed, were the unfortunate result of a civil war in which Muslims as well were killed. Official Turkish historians and their supporters worked tirelessly to turn an undeniable tragedy into a controversy, while Armenian and other scholars established a documentary record of archival materials, memoirs, and historical accounts to preserve the historical memory of official mass murder. For twentieth-century Armenians, particularly in the Diaspora, the Genocide of 1915 became the most potent source of their national identity, an ineradicable pain that remains unrecognized by much of the rest of the world.

The Ottoman Empire collapsed in the wake of World War I, as did the Russian Empire. Many Armenian survivors fled north to Russian Armenia, where on May 28, 1918, an independent republic was established, with Yerevan as its capital. This independent Armenia lasted only until the end of 1920. The first Armenian republic was a land of refugees, disease, and hunger. Some aid came from the United States, but famine was rampant in Yerevan. Isolated and insecure, independent Armenia had to fight all its neighbors to establish its borders. The Dashnak Party managed to organize elections, however, and a relatively representative government ran the country. The expectation that military aid would come from Europe or America never materialized, and ultimately Armenia was abandoned by the Allies.

The United States Senate rejected a request by President Woodrow Wilson that the Americans establish a protective mandate over Armenia. Threatened by the nationalistic Kemalist movement in Turkey, the Dashnak government agreed on December 2, 1920 to turn the new state over to Communists as the lesser danger to Armenian existence.

With Western Armenia in the hands of the triumphant Kemalists, only Eastern Armenia, that small portion of historic Armenia that had been under Persian rule until 1828 and then part of the Russian Empire until 1917, remained under the control of Armenians. The country was at the nadir of its modern history. By 1920 only 720,000 lived in Eastern Armenia, a decline of thirty percent. In the seven years of war, genocide, revolution, and civil war (1914-1921), Armenian society had in many ways been "demodernized," thrown back to its pre-capitalist agrarian economy and more traditional peasant-based society.

## Soviet Era

After an initial period of harsh rule, the Soviet Armenian government introduced the more moderate economic program known as NEP (the New Economic Policy), which denationalized much of the economy and gave the peasants the right to control their own grain surpluses. The leader of the Russian Communists, Vladimir Lenin, called this new policy a tactical retreat to "state capitalism."

In the view of supporters of Soviet Armenia the new republic provided a degree of physical security that Armenians had seldom known in their long past. Armenia was part of the largest country in the world, a Great Power that could easily prevent incursions from Turkey or Iran. But, in the view of the opponents of Soviet Armenia, the state was a fraudulent homeland that did not represent the national aspirations of Armenians. The Soviet government would not push the "Armenian Agenda" and attempt to retrieve lost lands in Turkey. Indeed, the Soviets had granted to the neighboring republic of Soviet Azerbaijan the Armenian-populated region of Nagorno Karabagh. Soviet Armenia was recognized by only a minority of the Armenians living outside the Soviet Union, and for decades many Diaspora Armenians spoke as if no Armenian state existed. The Diaspora and the Armenians within the Soviet Union grew distant from each other, with very little direct knowledge of how the other half was developing.

Stalin, who ruled with little opposition from roughly 1928 until 1953, established the rigid authoritarian political system and state-run economy that lasted until the fall of the Soviet Union. Anything that was suspected of nationalism was attacked and could condemn its author to prison. The Armenian Church was ruthlessly disciplined and made subordinate to the Soviet authorities. This led to disaffection among diasporan Church members, and a schism eventually divided the international Armenian Church. Some churches recognized the direct and exclusive authority of the Holy See of Echmiadzin, which lay in Soviet Armenia, while others rejected any but formal association with the Catholicos at Echmiadzin and gave their loyalty to a rival See at Antelias in Lebanon. The Cold War and the Iron

Curtain led to a deep division between Armenians, both within the Diaspora and between the Diaspora and the Armenians of the Soviet Union.

During World War II, the Soviet state and the Armenian Church made an uneasy peace. In its desperate struggle for survival, the Soviet government quickly made a number of concessions to the Armenian Church, which became the major link between Soviet Armenia and the Diaspora. In late 1942 some of the closed churches in Armenia were reopened, and exiled clergy returned from Siberia. The interests of the Church, the Armenian Diaspora, and the Soviet government most closely coincided in the brief interlude between the end of World War II and the onslaught of the Cold War. Stalin made claims to historic Armenian lands across the border in Turkey. Shortly after the Yalta Conference, the Soviet government initiated a campaign to encourage Armenian settlement in the Armenian republic and to recover Armenian irredenta in eastern Turkey. But the advent of the Cold War and Turkey's integration into the United States-led Western alliance made any border change impossible.

The Church supported the Soviet claims and encouraged the efforts to "repatriate" Diaspora Armenians to the Soviet republic. Tens of thousands migrated to Armenia, only to find an impoverished country with no political freedom. Some of them were exiled from their new homeland to prison camps in Siberia. A bitter anecdote of the time told of a repatriate who told his relatives and friends before migrating to Soviet Armenia that he would send them a photo of himself on arrival. If he was standing, things were good and they should also come to Armenia; if he was sitting, things were bad and they should stay where they were. When the photo arrived, the man was lying on the ground!

With the death of Stalin in 1953, life became easier in the USSR. The worst aspects of political terror ended, and though the monopoly of Communist party power remained, there was a significantly greater degree of social and cultural freedom in the years that Nikita Khrushchev ruled the Soviet Union (1953-1964). This period of reform, known as "the Thaw," improved the material and social life of the Armenians. Visitors from abroad became more common in Yerevan, and many Soviet Armenians moved from communal to private apartments. While the standards of living lagged far behind the most developed countries in the West, Armenians were able to meet their needs and many of their desires through the semi-legal "second economy."

The long stolid years of Leonid Brezhnev's rule (1964-1982) provided a stable, secure life for Armenians, but the arteries of the system were hardening. Corruption and cynicism increased, and few Armenians believed in the goals of the Communists. Along with new interest in the ordinary material amenities of normal life, Armenians comforted themselves with a renewed interest in their own history and culture, and nationalism became a unifying sentiment among both intellectuals and ordinary folk. While a quiet official commemoration of the fiftieth anniversary of the Armenian Genocide (April 24, 1965) took place in the Opera

House, thousands of Armenians demonstrated without permission in the streets of Yerevan. They called on Moscow to return Armenian lands to Armenia. Even the revered Catholicos of All Armenians, Vazgen I, had difficulty trying to calm the crowds. The Kremlin reacted by removing the head of the Armenian Communist Party, but eventually it agreed to have an official monument to the Genocide built on the high hill of Tsitsernakaberd.

Armenian nationalism had its roots in the long textual tradition that Armenian clerics and scholars had elaborated ever since the invention of the Armenian alphabet in the fifth century. While the Soviet regime was ostensibly anti-nationalist, in fact Soviet nationality policies contributed to a powerful feeling of territorial nationalism. Soviet Armenians were better educated, and knew their history, language and culture more thoroughly than most of their predecessors. Once the heavy hand of Stalin's terror was replaced by the greater tolerance of the late 1950's and 1960s, the pent-up demand for greater national and personal expression exploded in the form of a new nationalism.

Mikhail Gorbachev became General Secretary of the Communist Party of the Soviet Union in March 1985 and soon initiated his own revolutionary changes that eventually destroyed the USSR. Armenians reacted to the new liberal atmosphere by organizing a broad-based national movement by 1988. At first it focused on ecological issues. The transformation of Armenia into an industrial-urban country had brought in its wake severe ecological problems, most importantly the threat from a nuclear plant at Metsamor. But soon many Armenians expressed anger at the pervasive corruption and arrogance of the local Communist regime. Finally and most importantly, Armenians were concerned about the fate of Karabagh, the Armenian-populated enclave that lay in the Azerbaijani republic. Demonstrations both in Karabagh and Armenia in February 1988 led to a violent response from Azerbaijanis in the industrial town of Sumgait. More than two dozen Armenians were killed and a cycle of violence began that escalated over the next few years into a full-scale shooting war between the two republics.

## Independence

In the elections of the spring and summer of 1990, non-Communists won a parliamentary majority. After several rounds of voting, the newly elected Armenian parliament chose Levon Ter Petrosian instead of the Communist chief as its chairman. With the Pan-Armenian National Movement (HHSh) in power and the Communists in opposition, Armenia began a rapid transition from Soviet-style government to an independent democratic state. The following year, on September 21, 1991, Armenia declared itself independent of the Soviet Union.

The first years of the second independent republic were a time of nationalistic enthusiasm and extravagant hope for a prosperous, secure future. A parliamentary democracy with an elected president was established. By the spring of 1992 Armenian paramilitary forces had taken control of Karabagh, and despite some setbacks the Armenians essentially won the war with Azerbaijan by 1994, when a

The Land and People

cease-fire was declared. At this time there were signs that the government was becoming more authoritarian. Some newspapers were suppressed, and the major opposition party, the Dashnaktsutiun, was banned. In July 1995 a new constitution providing for an extremely strong presidency was adopted.

Ter Petrosian was reelected to the presidency the following year, but the outcome was disputed and he became far weaker and less popular than he had been. Nevertheless, he decided to try to break the impasse on peace in Karabagh. He proposed a bold compromise solution that would leave Karabagh formally within Azerbaijan while retaining the fullest possible autonomy and self-government for the local Armenians. Even his closest political allies turned against him, forcing his resignation in February 1998. New elections confirmed Robert Kocharian, formerly the leader of Karabagh, as Armenia's second president. Within a short time, two other politicians emerged as the most influential in Armenia – Vazgen Sargsian, the minister of defense and later prime minister; and Karen Demirjian, the former Communist party boss, who was, by the late 1990s, the most popular leader in Armenia. Sargsian and Demirjian allied in the elections of 1999 and won handily. But before they were able to carry out their policies, they were assassinated in the parliament building in October 1999. In the uncertain political environment at the end of the millennium, Kocharian once again emerged as the most powerful leader in Armenia.

Armenia's future appears at the moment, as in many times in its past, quite uncertain. The small republic is once again isolated, economically strapped, and discouraged. But one is reminded of other moments of Armenia's long history – of the early Christian era when it was between Byzantium and Persia; of the long centuries after the fall of the last Armenian kingdoms; of the years of genocide and dispersion in the early twentieth century. At each of these moments, Armenians revived and reconstructed their society, restored their cultural traditions, and reconceived their future.

The themes of Armenian history remain regeneration and survival, hope and faith in the darkness of the present. Knowing and appreciating the heroic efforts that this small people have made through time allows a degree of optimism about the years to come.

*Ronald Grigor Suny, Ph.D., is a professor of Political Science at the University of Chicago, and the author of several books, including* Looking Toward Ararat: Armenia in Modern History *(Indiana University Press, 1993).*

*Photograph: Dancing in traditional clothes on New Years Eve, Khor Virap, R. Kurkjian*

**Central Yerevan:**

Cascade (1); Mother Armenia Statue and Victory Park (2); Presidential Palace (3); Parliament (4); US Embassy (5); Matenadaran (6); Zoravar Church (7); Opera Square (8); Katoghike Church (9); Pedestrian Tunnel to Hrazdan Canyon (10); Yerevan Brandy Company (11); St. Gregory the Illuminator Cathedral (12); Farmer's Market (13); Sports Complex (14); Kilikia Central Bus Station (15); Tsitsernakaberd (Genocide Memorial), 16; Metro Stations (M)

# Yerevan Guide

When Yerevan celebrated the 2,780th anniversary of its founding a couple of years ago, it was finally possible for a person to know the city's age without using a calculator or doing the arithmetic on a piece of paper. The number 2,780 was on billboards and banners all over the city.

The name Yerevan is derivative of Erebuni, the Urartian settlement that was started by King Argishti around 782 BC. A fortress and other remains from the settlement are preserved at its site, on a hilltop just south of the modern city. In fact, Armenians today believe themselves to be descendants of the ancient Urartians.

For such an ancient city, its infrastructure and buildings are surprisingly youthful. With very few exceptions, the architecture that has survived is from the Soviet era. The street design dates back only to the 1920s, when architect Alexander Tamanian was called upon to create a modern Soviet city. He opted for broad avenues and expansive public spaces. As a result, there are none of the narrow and winding roads that you might expect in such an ancient settlement. The streets in the central city are instead arranged in concentric circles that are crossed by major avenues.

The construction material for most structures is the locally mined tuff, a stone that frequently has a pink hue and which gives the city's buildings a uniform appearance.

The focal point of the city is, by design, Republic Square, which is the location of many government offices, the state museum, and the country's grandest hotel—the one where the foreign visitors stayed during Soviet times. Azatutian Square, also known as Opera Square, is another famous location. This is one of the city's great meeting places, and it is a popular site for political rallies and stump speeches. During the past few years the people that have gathered here have been mostly interested in socializing at the many new cafes that have popped up.

On a clear day, however, it would be difficult to deny that the genuine focal point of Yerevan is Mt. Ararat, the twin-peaked mountain that dominates the southwest skyline. Clear days are not common here, however. The reason is Yerevan's geography, which looks something like a soup bowl. The city sits at the bottom of the bowl, encircled by hills. In the summer months, this often creates hazy conditions that block the view.

M. Karanian                                    *On Tamanian Street in Yerevan*

## USEFUL INFORMATION

### SAFETY

Violent street crime is almost unheard of in Yerevan, and there are no areas that one needs to avoid in order to avoid crime, even at night. Your greatest risk, instead, is from the automobile traffic. Pedestrians are rarely granted the right of way, even when they are walking with a green signal. Use extreme caution when crossing a street, *especially* when walking in a designated crosswalk. Pedestrians aren't saints, either. Jaywalking is common in the city, and the traffic can often become unruly.

Wild dogs have been a problem in Yerevan, especially late at night when they sometimes travel in packs. The number of these dogs has decreased in the past couple of years, but you should still use caution to avoid these dogs if you are walking alone at night.

Petty and nonviolent theft is probably the city's must common crime. Don't become paranoid, but don't leave valuables laying around unattended, either.

### MONEY

Yerevan has a cash economy, but there are some limited opportunities for using credit cards. Visitors should bring enough cash for their entire stay, or make arrangements for wire transfers for lengthy visits.

*Central Yerevan*                                                R. Kurkjian

## ATM Machines

ATM machines are still a novelty in Yerevan. There are now several of them, however, and many of them offer a choice of US or Armenian currency. You will find 24-hour machines operated by **HSBC Bank Armenia** at: (1) the lobby of the main office of the HSBC bank, which is located at 9 Sargsian Street, next to Hotel Armenia (Tel. 58-70-88; 58-70-95); (2) the lobby of the Komitas branch of the HSBC bank, which is located at 3 Komitas Ave. (Tel. 22-25-96; 22-87-57); (3) a kiosk on the corner of Baghramian Ave. and Moskovian Street; (4) near the Yeritasardakan metro station at 27 Abovian Street; and (5) in the lobby of the Hotel Armenia, on Republic Square next door to the main office of the HSBC bank. PLUS and GlobalAccess cards are accepted, but CIRRUS is not. You can also get a cash advance on a MasterCard or Visa, for a hefty fee. **Agrobank** operates ATM machines in the lobby of Hotel Erebuni and in the lobby of the Hotel Shirak, both of which are just off Republic Square.

## Banking and Wire Transfers

The leading foreign bank is HSBC. Accounts can be maintained there in either Armenian dram or in US dollars. Located at 9 Sargsian Street, next to Hotel Armenia. **Western Union** offers wire transfers to and from Armenia, and they maintain offices throughout the city, including at 2 Nalbandian Street, near Republic Square (Tel. 53-90-29). **Wells Fargo Bank** (www.wellsfargo.com) provides money transfers from the US directly to HSBC in Armenia. They can be reached in the Los Angeles area at 535 North Brand Blvd., Glendale, CA (Tel. 818-550-5021).

# INTERNET

Visitors who want access to the internet can either bring their own laptop computers or choose from the many internet cafes in central Yerevan. Access is available through the local phone service and is therefore only as reliable as your telephone line. This means that disconnects are common, and it may take several attempts before you can even get online.

If you are using your own computer, you can find the latest local access numbers for AOL by going to the sign-on page and clicking the "Access Numbers" tab. Then select "Armenia" from the drop-down list that appears. The AOL local access numbers in Yerevan are 59-32-54; 60-61-46. There's no local toll charge, but AOL charges its own surcharge of about $6 for each hour in addition to its regular monthly fee.

If you are dialing from a hotel room, you can probably use a standard US-style phone jack. From an apartment or an older office, you may need an adaptor. If you can't find one in the US, try one of the **Zig Zag** electronics stores located at either 20 Sayat Nova Ave., (Tel. 55-27-57) or at 24 Mesrop Mashtots Ave. (Tel. 53-76-75). Most electrical outlets use European-style plugs, so you'll need an adaptor for this as well. And if your computer operates only on the standard US current, which is 110 volts, then you'll also need a voltage converter.

You can also get access to the worldwide web from one of the many Internet cafés in the city. These businesses tend to come and go, but three that have been around for more than a year are: **Arminco**, 50 Khanjian Street (Tel. 57-58-23); **Internet Café**, 29 Mesrop Mashtots Street; and **Eva**, 4 Sarian Street. Rates are 1,000 dram (about $2) for one hour of access.

There are several web sites offering English-language news about Armenia, most of which are offshoots of Diaspora newspapers. **Asbarez Online** is a popular one, which originates in Glendale, California (www.asbarez.com). The web site of the Armenian Embassy in the US has an extensive directory of links, and is a good place to start any search (www.armeniaemb.org).

For a free subscription news service, try **Groong**, which will send stories to your e-mail account. Each message contains an item related to Armenia, usually exactly as it appeared in its original publication. Subscribe by sending an e-mail to listproc@usc.edu. Type "subscribe Groong" in the subject heading.

# NEWSPAPERS AND BOOKS

*Noyan Tapan Highlights* is the only English-language newspaper in the city. It is published weekly in Yerevan, and costs 1,000 dram (about $2). The *Armenian International Magazine* (AIM) is an English-language monthly magazine that covers news from Armenia and the Diaspora. It's published in the US, and shipped to Yerevan, where single copies cost 1,000 dram (about $2). These are the only English-language periodicals that are regularly available in Yerevan. Street vendors generally sell only Armenian and Russian language periodicals.

**Noyan Tapan Bookstore**, on Republic Square, offers a handful of English-language books, and so do the vendors each weekend at the Vernissage. Don't expect to find what you want, however. Instead, bring from home any books or magazines that you will want to read.

## Libraries

The US Information Service (USIS) library at the US Embassy is available to US citizens, but only by appointment and only at limited times. Located at 18 Baghramian Street (Tel. 52-98-25). The American University of Armenia (AUA) has a library with many English-language titles. You do not need an appointment to visit, and it's open daily except Sunday. Located on the ground floor of the AUA building at 40 Baghramian Street (Tel. 27-32-98; 28-03-09).

## FILM FOR CAMERAS

**Color print film** is inexpensive and plentiful in Yerevan and you can have it processed at any of the dozens of shops throughout Yerevan. A roll of print film is about 2,500 drams (less than $5) and processing costs roughly half of what you might pay in the US. Printing quality varies, however, and we suggest that you process only one or two rolls at a time to protect yourself against loss. **Black-and-white print, color slide film, and APS film** are rarely available, however, and you should bring your own supply from home. The Uniserv photo shop (Tel. 56-01-86) at 32 Abovian Street in Yerevan usually has a small selection of consumer grade Kodak and Fuji slide film for 3,500 dram (less than $7). And as far as we know, this is the only shop that does same-day E6 processing for slides. Processing in sleeves is 4,000 dram (roughly $8) and mounts are an additional 50 dram (nine cents) each. Color slide film and E6 processing are also available at Photo Opera (1 Baghramian Street) and at Jupiter Photo (Proshian Street). Prices are comparable, but processing may take a few days.

## TELEVISION AND RADIO

Television provides the greatest access to news from overseas. The broadcast stations are all in Armenian or Russian, but satellite television provides access to CNN, MTV, and to the BBC World Service. Voice of America's radio broadcasts and international music, can be heard on **Hye-FM 91.1 FM**.

## TELEPHONE

The most reliable, and expensive, telephone services are available from the major hotels. The Business Centre at the Hotel Armenia charges about $4 each minute for calls to the US. Long-distance calls can also be made from post offices, where they are a little less costly. Try the large post office at Republic Square, the main office at 22 Sarian Street, or the branch located at the corner of Abovian Street and Sayat Nova Ave. These post offices also sell international phone cards, and the blue phone cards that allow you to make local calls from the new pay phones on the street. To use one of the old-style pay phones for a local call, you'll have to purchase a token from a nearby street vendor.

The **best international telephone rates** are available by using the international ATT or Sprint operators directly from your hotel room or apartment. For **ATT**, dial (**8-101-11**) to reach the international operator. Tell the operator you wish to bill the call to your ATT calling card. To use your Sprint calling card, call the international **Sprint** operator by dialing (8-101-55). You can use these numbers to make **collect calls**, too.

To make an international call from a city in Armenia other than Yerevan, you will usually need to go to the main post office. In most cases you will also need to go to the post office to make a city-to-city call within Armenia.

To reach Yerevan from outside the country, dial (011) and then Armenia's **country code (374)** plus the Yerevan **city code (1)**. To reach Echmiadzin dial the country code (374) plus the Echmiadzin city code (59). Gyumri's city code is (41).

Local telephone service is generally poor and some telephones may not work all the time. Cellular telephone service is available and it's usually more reliable, but service areas are limited primarily to Yerevan. You can rent a cell phone in Yerevan from a business called **Rent-A-Phone Armenia** (Tel. 55-99-80) (Internet: www.renta-phone.am). Rentals are offered by the day, week or month, and fees range from roughly $5 to $10 each day, plus airtime.

## MAIL

**Letters** and **postcards** sent to the US directly from a post office in Yerevan generally arrive within about two weeks. In 2002, the rate for a first class letter was 250 dram (about fifty cents), and the rate for a post card was 170 dram (about thirty-five cents). Sending packages to the US, however, is less reliable. Don't be surprised if a local asks you to carry a letter back to the States, so that you can mail it to a US destination from a US post office.

Mail delivery to addresses within Armenia is not reliable. Don't expect the Armenian post office to deliver anything that you really want to arrive at its destination inside Armenia, regardless of whether its origin is local or foreign. Still, if you wish to try, use Yerevan's main postal code, 375000, for general delivery.

If you wish to purchase stamps as souvenirs, the postal service operates a special office called **Namakaneesh** where you can purchase, at face value, individual or complete sets of mint stamps and other postal items. The supply here is greater than at any post office, and includes issues dating back several years. Located at 43 Mesrop Mashtots Ave., near the Matenadaran.

The private shipping company **DHL** was among the first entrants to the Armenian market, and they offer reliable and fast delivery both in and out of the country. Delivery time for a letter is about five days (Tel. 58-66-88). **Federal Express** also provides service (Tel. 57-46-86). When shipping heavy packages that do not require immediate delivery, it is more economical to use a cargo company such as **Jet Line**, 37 East Beach Ave., Inglewood, California 90301 (Tel. 310-419-7404) or the local Armenian company **Saberatour-Sevan**, 37 Hanrapetutian Street (Tel. 52-54-48). **Seaborne International** also ships cargo and they have offices in both Los Angeles and Yerevan. 11222 La Cienega Blvd., Suite 470, Inglewood, California 90304 (Tel.310-216-4225) (E-mail: sarlax@aol.com). In Yerevan they are located at 15 Deghatan St., near HSBC and the Central Bank (Tel. 9-42-21-64).

# MAPS

Pocket-sized tourist maps of Yerevan are widely available from hotels and gift shops. Yerevan's English-language newsweekly, *Noyan Tapan Highlights*, prints a map and a list of tourist services in its center spread. For a color map of the city, pick up a free copy of *Yerevan Guide*, an advertising brochure that also contains a listing of tourist sites. The brochure is distributed at most hotels.

A comprehensive road atlas is published by Noyan Tapan. The 96-page booklet measures 8" x 11" and costs about $12. You can purchase a copy at the Noyan Tapan office at 28 Isahakian Street (Tel. 56-19-05; Fax 52-42-79) (E-mail: contact@noyan-tapan.am) (Internet: www.noyan-tapan.am).

# LAUNDRY

For professional laundry service, try **Pyunic Laundry**, which is Armenia's only commercial and self-service Laundromat. Pyunic charges about $3 to wash and dry five kilograms of your laundry. Delivery is available. Hours: 9 am to 7 pm. This is the former Selena Laundry, located in a basement storefront at 50 Pushkin Street, near Mesrop Mashtots Ave. (Tel. 53-68-05). A second location opened in 2000 next door to the Pizza Di Roma Restaurant, on Tumanian Street.

Most hotels now offer laundry services, as well, although at much higher rates. A laundromat at the US Embassy was once open to US citizens, but is now available only to Embassy employees. **Lavanda** provides regular laundry service, and dry cleaning services, as well (Tel. 55-24-34).

*Yerevan*                                                               *R. Kurkjian*

## HOTELS AND PLACES TO STAY

Until recently, any traveler looking for a comfortable Western style hotel in Armenia had no choices. There was only Yerevan's Hotel Armenia. Today, thanks to a building boom that has created hundreds of new rooms, visitors can be more selective. Most hotels have both electricity and hot water 24 hours, and their prices generally include the government's 20 percent VAT, unless stated otherwise. These are the city's major hotels, categorized according to price and level of service, and then listed alphabetically within each category. If you are traveling independently, you can reserve a room by telephone, so that you'll have a guaranteed place to stay when you arrive. The high-end and moderate hotels have English-speaking staff, and they can provide transportation from the airport, too. The budget hotels usually do not have English-speaking staff. Please note: room prices are listed as a reference guide to what you can expect, and are not guaranteed.

### High-End

The country's flagship hotel is still the massive **Hotel Armenia**, which faces Republic Square in the heart of the city. In 2003 the hotel will be renamed the **Armenia Marriott Hotel Yerevan** to reflect its new ownership. **Amenities:** private bath, air conditioning, satellite television and phone in each room. Facilities include two restaurants, café, bar, health club and business services. Single $100; Double $130; Suite $200. Includes breakfast buffet. Handicapped access: four steps to main lobby, elevator to all floors. 1 Amiryan Street, at Republic Square (Tel. 59-90-00; 59-90-01) (E-mail: info@hotelarmenia.com) (Internet: www.hotelarmenia.com).

The **Astafian Hotel**, which opened in March 2000, is luxuriously appointed, although with a décor that is a bit nouveau riche. There are only nine rooms, but they're massive suites that are designed for entertaining guests. One even has a large boardroom style table and a china-filled cabinet. **Amenities:** private bath, air conditioning, café, bar, health club. More than half the hotel is devoted to a casino hall, dance club and banquet facility, and the atmosphere is geared toward adults rather than families. Suites: $120-150. Handicapped access: one step to the foyer, a small elevator to the upper floors. 5/1 Abovian Street, across from the Yerevan Hotel (Tel. 52-11-11; 52-85-53).

Yerevan's newest hotel, the 14-room **Avan Villa Yerevan**, is located high above the city center in a residential neighborhood. The luxury accommodations are designed to pamper guests with all of the traditional Western amenities, while also providing traditional Armenian décor. **Amenities:** private baths, fitness and business centers, air conditioning. Single $138; Suite $162. Located at Nork Marash, overlooking the city. (Tel. 54-78-88; Fax 54-78-77) (E-mail: tufhosp@arminco.com) (www.tufenkian.am).

**Hotel Aviatrans** is new and clean, but a bit dark in mood. **Amenities:** private bath, air conditioning, satellite television and phone in each room. Single $75; Double $75 to $140. Includes breakfast. Handicapped access: one step to main lobby, elevator to all floors. Abovian Street, just steps from Republic Square (Tel. 56-72-26; 56-72-28; Fax 58-44-42) (E-mail: hotel@arminco.com).

**Hotel Bass** was the first of the new hotels to open in Yerevan. In just a few years it has earned a good reputation for service and comfort, and it has become a favorite choice among people traveling on business for the US government. The hotel is small, with only 14 rooms, but the rooms are spacious. **Amenities:** private bath, air conditioning, satellite television for an extra fee, and phone in each room. Facilities include restaurant, bar, sauna and business services. Single $120; Double $185. Includes breakfast. Handicapped access: stairs to all levels, no elevator. 3 Aigedzor Street, just off Proshian Street (Tel. 26-41-56; 22-13-53).

**Metropol** earns the dubious distinction as the most expensive and the worst value among all the hotels. The location near the Cognac factory isn't the best, either. Single $150; Double $250. 2/2 Mashtots Ave. (Tel. 54-37-01; Fax 54-37-02).

**Hotel Yerevan** opened in May 2000 and quickly became known as one of Armenia's finest. There are 104 rooms, many of them fairly small, and 20 spacious suites. **Amenities:** private bath (no tubs), air conditioning, satellite television and phone in each room. Facilities include a spacious atrium lobby and lounge, as well as an Italian restaurant, bar, exercise room, business services, and a rooftop swimming pool and sundeck. If you're not a hotel guest, you can use the swimming pool for a monthly membership fee of $150. Single $150; Double $185; Suites as high as $700. Prices do not include 20 percent VAT. Handicapped access: steps to main lobby, elevator to all floors. 14 Abovian Street, in the heart of the city (Tel. 58-94-00; Fax 56-46-77) (E-mail: yerhot@arminco.com) (Internet: www.hotelyerevan.com).

## Moderate

**Ani Plaza Hotel** had operated for years as the dismal Hotel Ani. A major renovation has made it one of the city's best, and its management has made it one of the best values, as well. **Amenities:** private bath (no tubs), air conditioning, satellite television and phone in each room. Facilities include a comfortable lobby with a lounge, gift shop and travel agency, as well as business services. Economy Single $70; Deluxe Double $145. Includes breakfast. Handicapped access: several steps to main lobby, elevators to all floors. 19 Sayat Nova Ave., at the corner of Abovian Street in the city center (Tel. 59-45-00; Fax 56-53-43) (E-mail: info@anihotel.com) (Internet: www.anihotel.com).

**Maison d/Hote de Nork** is an affordable option just outside central Yerevan, with a view of Mt. Ararat. **Amenities:** private baths, twin beds in all rooms. Single $50; Double $70. 123 Amaranotzayin St. (Tel. 65-39-49; Cell. 9-40-12-59).

**Hotel Sil** is located in a commercial zone just outside the center of the city. The location is not ideal, but the luxuriously appointed rooms, all at reasonable rates, are an appropriate consolation. **Amenities:** modern bath (no tubs), remote controlled air conditioning, television, phone, terry bathrobes. Facilities include a tiny spa-like swimming pool in the basement, sauna, exercise room, and a restaurant. Single $70; Double $94; Deluxe $150. Includes breakfast. Handicapped access: several steps to main lobby, elevator to all floors. 20 Tigran Mets Ave., near the outdoor markets (Tel. 54-07-08; 54-07-09; Fax 54-50-00) (E-mail: silhtl@arminco.com) (Internet: www.sil.am/hotel/index.htm).

Business travelers are lured to **Hye-Business Hotel Suites** by the lodge's emphasis on business services such as rooms with large desks, reading chairs and high-speed Internet access. **Amenities:** fully applianced kitchen, large desk, and a separate bedroom with private bath, air conditioning, cable television and phone, but economy accommodations are also offered. Studio $84; Standard $100; Deluxe $135. Handicapped access: stairs to all rooms, no elevators. 8 Hanrapetutian Street, near the United Nations Headquarters (Tel. 56-75-67; Fax 54-31-31).

## Budget

**Crown Hotel** is tiny and easily overlooked. Hot water in the morning and at night. Single $40; Double $50. 8 Abovian Street, near Republic Square (Tel. 58-98-79).

The **Hotel Dvin** renovated its 240 rooms recently, but improvements are difficult to detect. **Amenities** are few and the facilities are vintage Soviet. Hot water in the morning and evening only. Single $50; Double $60. Handicapped access: several steps to main lobby, elevator to all floors, steps in common areas. 40 Paronian Street, overlooking the Hrazdan canyon (Tel. 53-48-63; 53-63-43; Fax 15-19-28).

**Erebuni Hotel** is another of the city's old Soviet-era hotels, one which hasn't been renovated. Floor ladies keep an eye on things, and the hot water runs only in the morning and at night. But the low room rates and central location compensate for the poor service and musty smell. A sign clearly acknowledges that foreigners pay more than locals for the same rooms. Single $30; Double $40. Handicapped access: several steps to main lobby, elevator to all floors. 26 Nalbandian Street, behind Republic Square (Tel. 56-49-93; Fax 58-38-15).

The **Hotel Hrazdan**, until recently, was used as office space but has now been returned to service for travelers. The single rooms are a bargain for solo travelers, but the other rates are a bit pricey. Hot water in the morning and at night. Single $55; Double $90; Deluxe $115. 72 Zohrapi Street, just off Paronian Street and astride the Hrazdan canyon (Tel. 53-53-32; 54-00-09)(E-mail: asimon@freenet.am).

**Hotel Shirak** is also a good value in a no-frills hotel. Hot water in the morning and at night. Single $30. Handicapped access: elevator to all floors. 13 Movses Khorenatsi Street, one block south of Republic Square (Tel. 52-99-15).

**Foreign Students Guest House** offers hostel-style lodging with no frills. Each room has as many as five beds, each of which is rented out individually for about $20. 52 Mashtots St., in the center of the city. (Tel. 56-00-03) (E-mail: pr-int@ysu.am).

## Guest Houses

**Apartments** are available to visitors for both short and long term rentals. Rates are typically from $10 to $20 each night for an apartment with two or three rooms. Electricity is generally included in the rental, but if there's a satellite television you will be expected to pay for the service. The quality of the apartments varies widely. Many will not have 24-hour supplies of water, and air conditioning is unlikely. Owners have been known to stop by unexpectedly and often, for a myriad of reasons. But this is an affordable option for travelers with families. Handicapped access: varies. The elevators in many buildings are broken, and those that have been repaired are generally located at the top of at least one-half flight of stairs.

Many local travel agents can help you locate a suitable apartment. For assistance, try: Odette Aghabegians of **Menua Tours** (Tel. 52-73-72; Fax 58-39-01) (E-mail: info@menuatours.com) (internet: www.menuatours.com); or Sisak Abramian of **Tourism Management** (Tel. 22-41-11; Fax 27-73-44) (Internet: www.armasta.am).

For an excellent value try the small housing compound on the grounds of the **International Committee for the Red Cross (ICRC) Hospital**. The location just outside Yerevan on the Yerevan-to-Ashtarak highway is inconvenient, and you'll need a driver or a taxi for everything. But the accommodations are modern and European, and fairly-priced, too. Studio $18; 2-bedroom $30. Also available by the month for short-term rentals starting at $150 monthly. (Tel. 34-23-49; 35-32-97) (E-mail: archotel@freenet.am).

*Genocide Memorial at Tsitsernakaberd*          *M. Karanian*

Yerevan Guide

## Near Yerevan

**Pine Tree House** is a small bed and breakfast lodge located in Byurakan, which is in the foothills of Mt. Aragats, on the west side and not too far from the Byurakan Observatory. This is a good place to stay if you want to get a break from the heat of Yerevan or if you just want to be able to wake up in the foothills and go hiking. **Facilities** include hot showers and modern baths. Ask the proprietor, Mary Panian, about nearby horseback riding that is available. Single room $25. Breakfast included (Tel. 52-16-25).

## FOOD

*Khorovats*, which is a meal of barbequed pork, is certainly the most popular food in Yerevan. There's even a street that the locals have dubbed Khorovats Street because there's a khorovats stand every few feet. Its real name is Proshian Street, and this is a good place to look for a genuine barbecue dinner, prepared in a local atmosphere. Khorovats tastes great, but as with any food that you purchase on the street, you should use care when selecting a vendor, and ask for meat that is cooked thoroughly. **Subway:** Baghramian station, two stops north of Republic Square (Hanrapetutian Hraparak) station.

**Tipping** in restaurants is beginning to catch on, thanks to the Westerners who live or visit here. The norm for good service is ten percent of the bill, and some restaurants will add the gratuity onto the bill. Dining out is a leisurely activity. You will not be rushed on your way. You won't even get the check, unless you ask for it, even if you sit at your table all night. It would simply be too rude for most servers to encourage you to leave. There are plenty of traditional restaurants to choose from in Yerevan, too, and they offer international fare as well as traditional Armenian and Eastern dishes.

## Traditional Armenian and Middle Eastern

**Old Erivan Tavern** at 23 Tumanian Street offers a menu of tasty *kuftas*, *dolmas* and *kebobs*, all reasonably priced, to its mostly local clientele. We strongly recommend this restaurant. **Gold Star Bistro** and **Eastern Cuisine** are located next door to each other at 16 Komitas Street, and they offer similar menus that include chicken *kebobs* and *spas* (a yogurt-based soup that is served hot). Each of the restaurants is inexpensive, and popular with local residents. **Shahrazad**, which is located at 5 Amirian Street just a few doors from the Hotel Armenia, serves Arabic foods such as *humus* and *taboule*, all at reasonable prices. **The Alcon Café and Restaurant** at 15 Sayat Nova Street serves trout, *kebob*, *spas* and other traditional eastern foods. The atmosphere is upscale but the prices aren't. **Lebanon Cuisine** is located at 8 Khorhrdarani Street (Tel. 58-42-32), and has quickly become popular for its tasty *lahmahjoun*. **Dolmama** at 10 Pushkin Street (Tel. 56-89-31) serves *dolmas* and other traditional foods, mostly to Americans, at Western prices. The food and service is excellent, but we do not recommend this spot to anyone who is traveling on a budget.

## International

**Al Leoni** at 40 Tumanian Street (Tel. 53-83-31) serves gourmet Italian entrees and has a full bar that serves authentic cappuccino. The atmosphere and the prices are upscale. **Hotel Yerevan** at 14 Abovian Street (Tel. 58-94-00) also has fine Italian cuisine. For inexpensive pizza, try **Pizza Di Roma** or **Diamond Style Restaurant**, which are located

*Mt. Ararat*                                                          *R. Kurkjian*

side by side on Abovian Street near Republic Square. **Cactus** at 42 Mesrop Mashtots Ave. (Tel. 53-99-39) serves margaritas and Mexican food and is moderately priced. **Pepe's**, a restaurant at Hotel Armenia, also offers Mexican food. **Wheel Club** at 15 Parpetsi Street (Tel. 53-28-68) is popular with Americans, and is worth a visit for its international menu of American, English, Thai, Vietnamese and Cajun-style meals. In the past year, other international restaurants have opened, or were scheduled to open, featuring **Thai** (Baghramian Ave near Proshian St.); **French** (Khorhrdarani Street near Republic Square); **Chinese** (Tumanian Street) and **Indian** foods (Mesrop Mashtots Ave.).

## Fast food

There are fast food and burger joints just about everywhere, but few of them offer the quality of **Mr. Pig**, which is located on the corner of Abovian and Arami Streets, near Republic Square. There are several others on upper Abovian Street that are worth trying, including **California Pizza** at #21, **Charlie** at #26, and **Smak** at #52. **Queen Burger**, on Tigran Mets Ave., near the new cathedral, is also popular. None of the Western franchises are here, which makes Armenia one of the few countries in the world where the native cuisine hasn't been pushed aside by Ronald McDonald.

## Coffee and Dessert

For American style coffee and pastries you can try a typical donut shop such as **Yum Yum**, on 40 Mesrop Mashtots Ave. near the Cascade. The air conditioning makes this a great oasis during the summer months and it's a great place to meet other Americans. But for Armenian style coffee and traditional pastries such as baklava, check out any of the street cafes. For the best pastries and coffee, go where the locals go. In central Yerevan, that would be **Eresse Anatolia Patisseria**, at 116 Nalbandian Street (Tel. 58-57-38) at the corner of Sayat Nova Ave. The pastries are fresh, the coffee is strong, and the staff is friendly. **Lagonid Bistro Cafe**, at 37 Nalbandian (Tel. 58-49-93) also offers coffee and pastry.

For English tea, there's an authentic teahouse in the center of the city at 11 Abovian Street. This teahouse, **Natura Gold** (Tel. 56-90-91; 54-47-87), sells brewed tea by the pot or cup, and it sells tea leaves by the kilogram, as well.

Groceries

If you're shopping for food there is an abundance of small grocery stores to choose from throughout the city. Some of the better choices are: **Aroma**, located at the corner of Sayat Nova Ave. and Nalbandian St.; **SAS**, which offers home delivery, located at 18 Mesrop Mashtots Ave. near Amirian Street (Tel. 56-33-99); and **Partez**, which was the first of the Western-style markets, and is located on 16 Vagharshian Street, near Komitas Ave. **Aragats** was one of the first stores in Yerevan to remove the barricades that separated customers from the goods, and customers are allowed to touch grocery items without asking for permission. The clerks who aggressively follow customers throughout the store mitigate this convenience, however. This store is located at 1 Tamanian Street near the Cascade. You'll be able to find many Western brands at each of these stores.

Two large food markets, known as *shukas*, feature vendors who sell fresh produce, meat, dried fruit, fresh bread and homemade *matsun* (yogurt). There's usually someone selling live chickens and turkeys, too. These markets are still the primary food sources for most Armenians, despite the recent arrival of some small Western style grocery stores. The main *shuka*, located on Mesrop Mashtots Street, has been fading in popularity lately. But there's a huge shuka, on Tigran Mets Street that is thriving and worth a visit even if you're not shopping for anything. Look for it across the street from the metro station, and next to the large department store. Some neighborhoods also have small farmers' markets that sell greens, fruits, vegetables, and sometimes dairy products such as fresh *matsun*.

## ATTRACTIONS/SIGHTSEEING

Yerevan is a tourist's delight. The streets are arranged in a compact and concentric pattern that makes it easy to walk just about everywhere. And those locations that are difficult to reach by foot are still only a 1,000-dram (less than $2) cab fare away. Subway station stops are listed whenever a station is nearby.

Start your tour by taking a cab to the massive monument honoring **Mother Armenia** where you will have great views of the city that you are about to traverse by foot. The statue of Mother Armenia stands sentry over Yerevan, and sometimes appears to be directly in line with Mesrop Mashtots Street. The statue is actually located in **Victory Park**, which occupies a hilltop overlooking the center of the city. The park and the statue are both worth a visit, and will provide a vantage point from which to view all of Yerevan. There's a Ferris wheel and several carnival rides at the park, as well as a small artificial lake where you can rent a rowboat. Inside the base of the Mother Armenia monument is a museum dedicated to war veterans.

Armenia commemorated its fiftieth year as a Soviet Republic with a nearby monument at the top of the **Cascade**. To reach the Cascade from Victory Park, cross the street at the park's main entrance and walk south about 50 yards. The city center is located hundreds of steps below. Athletes sometimes run up the steps for exercise, but the greatest attraction of these steps to tourists is the view from the top, especially at sunset. Construction of this monument of white steps was halted several years ago when money ran out, so the top quarter of it is unfinished. Still, the site is open and it's possible to traverse its full expanse with only a brief detour. At the base you can rest at one of several cafes, and visit the statue of Alexander Tamanian, the architect of Yerevan. A comprehensive project to complete the Cascade steps, and to build an art museum on an adjacent parcel of land, has been funded by an Armenian-American philanthropist. Site work is expected to be underway by 2003.

The **Matenadaran** houses an impressive collection of ancient manuscripts and is probably Armenia's most famous museum. The building is just a five-minute walk from the base of the Cascade. The documents at the museum provide insight into Armenia's historical, scientific, literary and artistic development over the ages, and make the Matenadaran the most important site on any city tour.

The building is also home to the Matenadaran Scientific Research Institute, an important library for academic research. There are more than 14,000 Armenian manuscripts at the museum, and another 2,500 from foreign sources. Only about one percent of them are on display to the public at any time, but even that one percent is enough to make this a world-class museum that warrants a special visit.

Self-guided tours are permitted, but you're apt to overlook the significance of many items if you rely only upon the signs for guidance. English-speaking tour guides are available, and will make your visit more meaningful. Admission and the tours are free, but donations are accepted. Reservations are not needed, but large groups should call beforehand. Open 10 am to 4 pm daily except Sunday and Monday. Located at 53 Mesrop Mashtots Street, at the top of the street (Tel. 56-25-78; 58-32-92) (Internet: www.matenadaran.am). **Subway:** Yeritasardakan station, one stop north of Republic Square (Hanrapetutian Hraparak) station.

**Azatutian Hraparak**, which is also called the **Opera Square**, is a short walk from the base of the Cascade, across Moskovian Street, at the corner of Mesrop Mashtots Street and Sayat Nova Avenue. This is a popular public gathering place, in addition to being the location of the **National Opera House**. In summer months, children on skates and roller blades fill the park, competing for space with others who are playing ping-pong, or sipping Cokes at one of the square's cafes. This is the largest pub-

*Spandarian Reservoir in southern Armenia*                    *R. Kurkjian*

Yerevan Guide

lic space in the city center, and it was the location of many political rallies during the closing years of the Soviet Union, and throughout the 1990s. **Subway:** Yeritasardakan station, one stop north of Republic Square (Hanrapetutian Hraparak) station.

It is **Republic Square**, however, that is the heart of the city. During the Soviet era, military parades crossed the square and passed reviewing stands that were filled with the country's elite. Today, the square is still the site of national parades, although floats and balloons have replaced guns and rockets. This is also a popular gathering spot, for young people, especially after sunset during the hot summer months. The fountains pulsate, or dance say some, and help to cool the air. In the summer, it used to be common to see young children stripped down to their underpants, swimming in the fountain pools. During the past couple of years, however, the authorities have forbidden swimming.

This square, which is actually shaped more like an oval, is flanked by some of Armenia's most prestigious buildings. The **National Museum** occupies the most prominent location [see museum listings for details], and the fountains at the front of the building attract large crowds. Across the square, a green lawn occupies the spot where a statue of Lenin had once stood. A 40-foot-tall cross was installed here in December 2000 for ceremonies commemorating Armenia's 1700-year history of Christianity. Behind the green lawn there's a park filled with fountains and cafes. **Subway:** Republic Square (Hanrapetutian Hraparak) station.

Just a five minute walk from Republic Square is Yerevan's newest and largest cathedral. **The Cathedral of St. Gregory the Illuminator** is a massive structure that has been under construction for the past couple of years. It is scheduled for consecration in September 2001. It's located near the crossroads of Tigran Mets Ave. and Khanjian Street, south of Republic Square. In a nod to Armenia's celebration in 2001 of the 1700th anniversary of its adoption of Christianity, the church is designed to accommodate 1,700 parishioners. **Subway:** Zoravar Andranik station, one stop south of the Republic Square (Hanrapetutian Hraparak) station.

Just down the street from the cathedral is one of the city's largest **outdoor markets**. Vendors set up here on both sides of Tigran Mets Ave., but the more interesting location for visitors is the market on the east side of the street, which includes a huge indoor *shuka* (food market) as well. This isn't a tourist attraction, but is instead a genuine market that Armenians use every day. It offers a fascinating glimpse of one part of daily life in Yerevan.

Not on this walking tour, but of interest nevertheless, are a trio of religious sites. The tenth century monastery of **Katoghike** is centrally located, behind 15 Abovian Street, and is Yerevan's oldest religious center. Most of the building was destroyed during the Soviet era, to make way for state offices. One small part of the church complex was saved, however, and it abuts the new building. This remnant of the church is so small that many parishioners stand outside of it during the daily church services. If you visit, remember that this is a functioning church, so behave accordingly. Katoghike is not visible from the street. To find it, you walk behind that twentieth century office building on Abovian Street. **Zoravar Church**, which dates back to only AD 1693, is also hidden from the street, and located inside the block bounded by Moskovian, Pushkin, and Tumanian streets.

*Photograph: Outdoor concert in Yerevan, R. Kurkjian*

By comparison, the **Blue Mosque** on Mesrop Mashtots Street, which was built in the early 1700s, is almost modern. It had fallen into ruin during Soviet rule, but has been carefully rebuilt by Iranian benefactors during the past three or four years. The building and grounds are closed to visitors, but the minaret and the blue tile roofs are visible from the street, and they serve as a reminder that the rule of the Persian Empire had once been extended as far north as this city.

**Tsitsernakaberd**, site of the Genocide Memorial is too far away to include in a walking tour of the city, but this is probably appropriate. Visits to this memorial and museum are reverent, and should be made separately. The memorial is outdoors and may be visited at any hour. Twelve massive blocks of stone lean inward and surround an eternal flame. An obelisk stretches high to the sky in two parts that are separated by a fissure. The twelve stone blocks represent the provinces of western Armenia that were emptied of their native Armenian population. The obelisk symbolizes the union of western and eastern Armenia.

Tens of thousands of Armenians make a pilgrimage to the memorial each year on April 24, which is a national day of commemoration and mourning. The **Museum of the Armenian Genocide** is located nearby and is open Tuesday through Sunday (Tel. 39-09-81). The memorial and museum are located at **Tsitsernakaberd Park**, on a hill overlooking the city, just west of the Hrazdan Canyon.

Also too far to walk to, but right on the subway line, is an interesting statue of the legendary hero and leader **Sasuntsi David** and the city's major transportation hub for buses and trains. **Subway:** Sasuntsi David station, two stops south of Republic Square station.

## SHOPPING

The best places to shop for souvenirs and gifts are the outdoor markets that operate each weekend. The biggest of these is the **Vernissage**, which sets up in the pedestrian mall that connects Republic Square with Hanrapetutian Street. Here you will find artisans selling handcrafted backgammon boards, engraved stones, original paintings, woven dolls, and lace, from 10 am until about 4 pm each Saturday and Sunday. Other vendors offer old stamps and coins, samovars, used books and jewelry and carpets. **Subway:** Republic Square (Hanrapetutian Hraparak) station.

A group of artists have set up a specialty market just for original paintings at **Sarian Park**, which is located near Opera Square. Every weekend here you'll find a large selection of original oil, acrylic, watercolor, and pastel paintings. Paintings rarely carry a sticker price, so you'll be expected to negotiate for each purchase. The artists are of uneven abilities, but some of the work is outstanding. **Subway:** Yeritasardakan station, one stop north of Republic Square station.

For a more traditional shopping experience, there are several gift shops offering souvenirs and carpets, generally at fixed prices. Try **Salt Sack**, on 3/1 Abovian Street near Republic Square (Tel. 56-89-31), where the owner will also get you an export license to go with your carpet. Or try locally owned **Salon of Souvenirs**, at 6 Tamanian Street near the Cascade (Tel. 52-52-61). **Gor Souvenirs and Art Works**, 28 Moskovian Street (Tel. 52-32-50), sells original sculptures and other gift items.

Shops that specialize primarily in carpets are located on Amirian Street near the Hotel Armenia, and also on Tumanian and Abovian Streets.

A large selection of music is available on CD from several stores on Abovian Street. You'll frequently find traditional and modern music from Armenian and Russian artists for as little as 1,000 dram (about $2) for each CD. Computer software, some of it in English, is also available. Most of it, unfortunately, appears to have been bootlegged.

If you want to experience shopping the way the many locals do, check out the daily outdoor market near the **Hrazdan** stadium. Most of the vendors offer inexpensive clothing, but there are some electronics and kitchen appliances for sale, too. There's also an indoor bazaar that sells clothing on the top floor of the **Hayastan Market**. The market is located at the top of Baghramian Street. **Subway:** Barekamutiun station, three stops north of Republic Square station, and the last stop on the subway line.

Several boutiques and specialty shops have opened in recent years, selling Levis jeans, famous brands of sneakers, designer fashions and cosmetics. Many of them are located along fashionable Abovian Street. Prices at most of these stores are higher than one would pay in the US, and the selection is usually limited.

Specialty stores selling **Armenian brandy** seem to have popped up everywhere. One of the larger outlets, which has been in business for several years, is located at 45 Mesrop Mashtots Ave. Armenian brandy is the same product that was until recently known as Armenian cognac. The name was recently changed in deference to the French, but the quality is still superb. The greatest selection of these brandies is available for purchase directly from the distillery, the Yerevan Brandy Company, which is located just five minutes by car from the city center on Admiral Isakov Ave. They also offer free tours to those who call ahead to make arrangements (Tel. 52-68-91; 54-00-00). One of the highlights of the tour is the reserve room of 24,000 bottles, some of them one century old.

There are several varieties of locally produced **Armenian wine** available, too. Two of the most popular brands are Areni and Getap, which are made from grapes that are grown in the Areni and Getap region, near Yeghegnadzor.

## ENTERTAINMENT

For live classical entertainment, check with the box office at the Opera House, which is located at the Opera Square. There you will learn about scheduled performances of the **Yerevan Ballet Company** and the **Armenian Philharmonic Orchestra**. The ballet company performs on Sundays, as does the symphony orchestra. The **National Chamber Orchestra** performs at the Komitas Chamber Music Hall, located at 1 Isahakian Street (Tel. 52-67-18).

**Jazz** is popular in the city, and you'll find an abundance of bars and cafes that offer live performances. Some of the more popular spots include: **Crystal Bar and Café**, 24 Sayat Nova Ave.; **Luxor Café** and **Crystal Bar and Café**, which are both located just across the street; and the **Paplavok Jazz Café**, in the park near the corner of Abovian and Moskovian Streets.

**Folk music** and the music of the **duduk** are also popular. Performances are often scheduled at the **Komitas Chamber Music Hall**, 1 Isahakian Street (Tel. 52-67-18) and at the **Aram Khachaturian Music Hall**, 46 Mesrop Mashtots Ave (Tel. 58-34-71). Call for current schedules, or check the current edition of the *Yerevan Guide*, or *Noyan Tappan*, which are available at most hotels and gift shops.

**Dance Clubs** come and go with regularity, but a couple that have survived more than one season are the **Relax Dance Club**, 31 Moskovian Street (no cover, couples only) and the **Nostalgie**, on the top floor of the Youth Palace building, at the top of Terian Street (no cover, singles welcome). The **Omega Club**, Terian Street near Sayat Nova Ave., and **Pioneer Club**, 2 Baghramian Ave. (Tel. 58-18-19) offer dance shows.

**Gambling** is offered at many storefront casinos throughout the city. Most of these casinos are limited to a small room with slot machines that accept only tokens and pay out tiny jackpots. Larger halls, such as the **Gloria Casino** on Tumanian Street near Mesrop Mashtots Ave., also offer card games and roulette. The **Astafian Hotel** has a large casino hall among its many fine entertainment facilities. Located at 5/1 Abovian Street, across from the Yerevan Hotel (Tel. 39-52-11-11; 39-52-85-53).

As an alternative to casino slot machines, there are two **video arcades** in the central city. The **Khagheri Ashkhar Arcade**, on Abovian Street between Sayat Nova Ave. and Moskovian Street, has a large selection of games. Tokens are sold for 100 dram (about 20 cents) each. Another smaller arcade is located on Mesrop Mashtots Ave. near Tumanian Street.

## SPORTS AND RECREATION

Athletic facilities throughout Armenia are limited, and many are in poor condition. The reason is not a lack of interest, but rather a lack of funding. Still, there are several sporting diversions available to visitors in Yerevan. Subway station stops are listed whenever a station is nearby.

**Golf** is available just outside the city limits, at the ambitiously named **Ararat Valley International Golf Course**. Although there are plans for a standard nine-hole course, two tennis courts, and even a miniature golf course, golfers in 2002 will find only a 150-meter driving range. Still, this is the only known facility in the Caucasus, and it has a spectacular view of Mt. Ararat. Located ten minutes by car from central Yerevan, on the Ashtarak Highway. *Seasonal.*

**Swimming** is available indoors, and at limited times, at the hospital of the **International Committee for the Red Cross**. This trauma and rehabilitation center also allows limited public access to its modest exercise room, gym, and sauna. Passes, roughly $10 for one visit, must be purchased in advance at the Red Cross office in Yerevan. Located ten minutes by car from central Yerevan, on the Ashtarak Highway, and just across the road from the new driving range. *Open year round.*

**Hotel Yerevan** has a rooftop swimming pool and sundeck, which means that this is the best rooftop swimming pool and sundeck in the entire country. Even if you're not a hotel guest, you can use the swimming pool for a monthly membership fee of $150. 14 Abovian Street, in the heart of the city (Tel. 58-94-00; Fax 56-46-77) (E-mail: yerhot@arminco.com) (Internet: www.hotelyerevan.com). **Subway:** Republic Square (Hanrapetutian Hraparak) station.

**Water World** offers swimming and water sports at its vast outdoor park. In addition to the main pool, this Western-style facility offers water slides, a separate wading pool for children, beach chairs, showers, and a pavilion where live entertainment is sometimes scheduled. Admission prices are determined by one's height, but figure 6,000 dram (about $12) for an adult, 1,500 dram ($3) for a child, and free for toddlers. Located five minutes by car from central Yerevan, on Miasnikian Ave., also known as the Nork roadway. *Seasonal.* Open 11 am to 7 pm (Tel. 63-34-30).

**Tennis** courts are available for hourly rental at the **Ararat Tennis Club**, located on Alek Manukian Street near Nalbandian Street, in the park across from Yerevan State University. There's also a sport center located near the soccer stadium at the city's edge, where courts and playing fields are sometimes available to the public. **Subway:** Yeritasardakan station, one stop north of Republic Square station.

If all of this sporting activity results in routine **muscle aches and pains**, you can get a therapeutic massage for roughly $20 from one of the licensed practitioners at **Thai Massage**. A dry sauna and hot showers are also available. This clean and modern facility is located at 2 Baghramian Street, near Moskovian Street (Tel. 58-56-70).

For children, the best playgrounds and carnival style kiddy rides are available at the **Hrazdan Canyon Park** and at **Victory Park**. The park at the Hrazdan Canyon can be reached by a road opposite the Hotel Dvin, or through a tunnel that passes under Sarian Street, at the main post office. The cooling effect of the Hrazdan River makes this a great place to escape the heat of the city. It's also popular with early morning joggers.

During the summer, an amusement-park-style tour mobile carries passengers from the Malibu Café on Mesrop Mashtots Ave., through the tunnel and into the children's park in the Hrazdan Canyon. The fare is 100 dram (roughly 20 cents).

Victory Park, however, offers more amenities. The playground there is Yerevan's biggest, and has a Ferris wheel, bumper cars, rowboat rentals and slow rides for children. Victory Park is located near the top of the Cascade on the hilltop overlooking the central city. The park is also home to the statue of Mother Armenia, and it offers great views of the city. **Table tennis** is available here and at parks throughout the city.

The **National Zoo**, located on the Nork roadway near Water World, is poorly funded and should be avoided. The exhibit of **reptiles** at a hall on central Yerevan's Abovian Street, near the Moscow Theater building, is interesting, however.

**Yerevan Guide**

# THE ARTS

## Major Museums of History

**State Museum of Armenian History** (sometimes referred to as the National Museum), Republic Square between Abovian and Nalbandian Streets. An archaeological exhibit on the main floor features engraved stone crosses, or khatchkars, and artifacts from the Stone Age through the Medieval period. There are also native costumes, ancient coins, some interesting models of Yerevan and of the Zvartnots Cathedral, and a collection of maps. Of particular interest is a wall-sized map of Van that was handdrawn in 1920 by the artist and cartographer Martiros Kheranyan. A visit to this museum should be high on your Yerevan itinerary. Closed Mondays. Open 10 am to 6 pm Tuesday through Sunday. (Tel. 58-27-61)

**Museum of the Armenian Genocide**, Tsitsernakaberd Park, near the Genocide Memorial. The museum is built into a hillside in a dark, tomblike structure that evokes the unfathomable blackness of this national tragedy. It would be unthinkable to visit Armenia without making a pilgrimage to this hallowed site (Tel. 39-09-81)

**Matenadaran**, 53 Mesrop Mashtots Ave. An extraordinary collection of 14,000 ancient Armenian manuscripts is stored at this museum, of which roughly 200 or so are on public display. The oldest dates back to the fifth century. This building also houses the Matenadaran Scientific Research Institute, where scholars study the many documents that are not on display. This is cer-

R. Kurkjian                                                    State Museum of Armenian History

tainly Armenia's most significant museum and you would be foolish to miss it. English-speaking guides are available and we recommend that you use one so that your visit will be more meaningful. Open 10 am to 4 pm daily except Sunday and Monday. (Tel. 58-32-92) (www.matenadaran.am).

**Erebuni Museum**, 38 Erebuni Ave., just south of the city. Artifacts from the ancient settlement of 782 B.C. Perhaps more interesting is the fortress located on the same site. The site is of great historical significance, but ironically there isn't a lot to see. Still, it's worth a short visit if you have time (Tel. 45-97-11).

## Selected Art Museums

**National Art Gallery**, Republic Square, located on the top floors of the State Museum of Armenian History. Third largest collection in the former Soviet Union, and a rival to the Hermitage (Tel. 58-08-12)

**Museum of Modern Art**, 7 Mesrop Mashtots Ave. (Tel. 53-56-61). At the moment this is the leading modern art museum, but a new museum is planned for a vacant site near the Cascade. The new museum will be part of a major renovation of the Cascade.

**Museum of Sergei Parajanov**, 15/16 Dzoragyugh Street, overlooking the Hrazdan Gorge. Honors the famous movie director. Displays include sketches and materials pertaining to the films that Parajanov directed. Perhaps his most famous was "The Color of Pomegranates." (Tel. 53-84-73)

**Museum of Painter Martiros Sarian**, 3 Sarian Street. The studio of this famous painter is preserved on the second floor of the museum and there is a gallery of his work on the main floor. (Tel. 58-17-62)

**Museum of Poet-Writer Yeghishe Charents**, 17 Mesrop Mashtots Ave. The poet lived and worked here until his arrest. Displays feature his works, his studio. (Tel. 53-55-94)

**Museum of Composer Aram Khachaturian**, 3 Zaroubian Street. Home of the composer has been preserved as it was when Khachaturian lived here. Museum includes a concert hall. (Tel. 58-94-18)

**Children's Art Gallery of Armenia**, 13 Abovian St., near Tumanian. Large windows facing the street allow even passers-by the opportunity to view some of the artwork on display here. (Tel. 52-09-02)

**State Folk Art Museum**, 64 Abovian St. Featuring woodwork, carpets, pottery and more.

**Near East Museum** and the **Museum of Literature and Art**, both at 1 Aram Street, at the back entrance to the State Museum of Armenian History.

MUSIC HALLS

**Aram Khachaturian Music Hall**, 46 Mashtots Ave. (Tel. 58-34-71)

**Komitas Chamber Music Hall**, 1 Isahakian Street (Tel. 52-67-18)

**Municipal Music Hall**, 2 Abovian Street (Tel. 58-28-71)

**Sports and Concert Complex**, Tsitsernakaberd Park (Tel. 39-99-13)

**Paplavok Jazz Café**, 41 Isahakian Street (Tel. 52-23-03)

THEATERS

**National Opera and Ballet Theater of Armenia**, 54 Tumanian Street (52-79-92)

**Hrachia Ghaplanian Dramatic Theater**, 28 Isahakian Street (Tel. 52-47-23)

**Chamber Theater**, 58 Mashtots Ave. (Tel. 56-63-78)

**Hamazgain Theater**, 26 Amirian Street (53-94-15)

**Stanislavsky State Russian Drama Theater**, 54 Tumanian Street (Tel. 56-91-99)

There are, of course, many other cultural opportunities in Yerevan. This listing covers only the major sites that will appeal to most visitors. For additional listings, and for show times for the performing arts, pick up a copy of the *Noyan Tapan* weekly newspaper.

## ANCIENT MANUSCRIPTS

There's a book on display at the Matenadaran Museum that looks heavy enough to have broken the back of the person who lifted it into its case.

It's a massive tome that contains a collection of biographies, sermons, and historical passages, none of them completed later than AD 1202. The book is known as the Homilies of Moush and it just might be the unlikeliest of exhibits at this museum. In 1915, with the survival of the Armenian nation in peril, the Homilies was cut into two volumes by a couple of Armenian women who were fleeing the massacres. Both women, and thus both halves of the book, survived.

The stories behind many of the Matenadaran's other 16,700 manuscripts are more obscure. But historians are hopeful that their future will be less perilous than their past.

The Armenians have had a Matenadaran—the English-language translation of the word is depository—since the fifth century AD. Scribes painstakingly created manuscripts that told of religious or historical events, and they lavishly illustrated the pages with their original paintings. Today, scholars at the Matenadaran's Scientific Research Institute study the documents not only for their artistic merit, but also as contemporary accounts of history and of scientific achievements. The manuscripts often serve as primary research for historians.

The oldest of the remnant pages date back to the fifth century, which is perhaps not surprising inasmuch as the unique Armenian alphabet was developed in AD 405. The oldest intact manuscript that has survived is a seventh century Gospel. Museum curators mention a collection of historical and scientific works from AD 981 as one of their most signifcant holdings, however, and they cite the

Gospel of Lazarus, from AD 887, as a unique and priceless gem. There has also been an AD 1477 Armenian gospel from Karabagh on display in recent years.

Scribes often used parchment for these creations, and their sources for inks ranged from dead insects to genuine liquefied gold. The insects— small worms, actually—were pulverized to create a rich red ink. The gold was combined with garlic juice to make it adhere to the page. Some of the qualities and shades of these colors have eluded synthetic duplication, even today.

The collection at Yerevan's Matenadaran was originally gathered together in the 19th century at the seat of the Armenian Church in Echmiadzin. These documents were protected, but it's estimated that tens of thousands of rare manuscripts in Turkey were intentionally destroyed by Turkish authorities during the Genocide.

The surviving Armenian manuscripts remained at Echmiadzin until 1959, when they were moved to their present location. Their modern home in Yerevan is a museum that looks like a giant vault and which is built into the side of a hill. Today, the Matenadaran is identified by the author Philip Marsden as a shrine to the Armenian language and the heart of the nation. A statue of Mesrop Mashtots, the inventor of the Armenian alphabet, greets visitors at the front entrance. Several khatchkars (engraved stone crosses) are displayed here, as well.

Stored deep in a vault, roughly 16,500 of the museum's 16,700 manuscripts have been preserved, and are awaiting further study. The rest are on display to the public, alongside that massive book that two peasant women managed to save.

# VOLUNTEER ACTIVITIES

A great way to add meaning to your visit to Armenia or Karabagh is to work as a volunteer. The **Peace Corps** (www.peacecorps.gov) operates in Armenia but they have a policy against allowing volunteers to select a particular country, so you could end up just about anywhere. You might instead wish to assist one of the groups listed below.

The **Land and Culture Organization** (Tel. 212-689-7811) (E-mail: lcousa@aol.com) (Internet: www.lcousa.org) is a US-based organization that renovates ancient monuments. Many of the volunteers are college students on their summer breaks. Write: PO Box 1386; Hoboken, NJ 07030. **Habitat for Humanity** organizes volunteer opportunities in partnership with **Habitat Armenia** (Tel. 800-422-4828 ext. 2549) (Internet: www.habitat.org/GV).

The **Fund for Armenian Relief (FAR)** sponsors the **Armenian Volunteer Corps** (E-mail: jasondemerjian@yahoo.com) (Internet: www.armenianvolunteer.org). Projects range from promoting public health in Karabagh to helping small business development in Armenia. **Pyunic** (Tel. 56-07-07) (E-mail: pyunic@arminco.com) is an association for the disabled that will accept volunteer workers. They can be reached in the US at 6606 Cantaloupe Ave., Van Nuys, CA 91405 (Tel. 818-785-3468).

Forestation is the object of the **Armenian Tree Project** (Tel. 56-99-10; 55-30-69) (E-mail: atp@ultranet.com). In the US they can be reached at 160 Second Street, Suite 250, Cambridge, Mass. 02142 (Tel. 617-492-2900)

In Yerevan, children who might otherwise fall through society's cracks are helped at the **Orran Center** (Tel. 53-55-90). The children receive guidance, they're helped with their studies, and they also get a hot meal every weekday. Located on Arami Street, which is the pedestrian mall near the Sarian Street post office. In Tsaghkadzor there's a **Children's Camp** (Tel. 0-23-52-70; 0-23-53-70) that accepts volunteers. Located in Tsaghkadzor, about a thirty-minute drive from Yerevan, in a beautiful forested location.

*Photograph: Poppy field bathing in sun, R. Kurkjian*

# Regional Guide

*The monasteries have been the pillars of the country, the fortresses against the enemy, and shining stars.*

**–Nerses the Gracious**

Armenia is a small country, and Yerevan is centrally located, so you might think that you can see the whole place as easily as you might be able to take a tour of, say, Maryland, which is roughly the same size. Not so. There are no super-highways, and many of the roads, although in good condition, wind through mountains, or pass through towns, resulting in slow going. Checking the mileage to a destination will not always give you an accurate indicator of how long it will take to get there.

This section treats Yerevan as a launching point for your travels, and lists the nearby regional sights that you can easily see in a day or less, and still return to your hotel or apartment in Yerevan. Other destinations that either require an overnight stay, such as Goris in the far south, or destinations that *deserve* an overnight stay, such as Lake Sevan and Dilijan, are treated separately.

It is difficult to find bottled drinking water for sale outside Yerevan, so when traveling outside the city always take enough fresh water for the entire trip. If you forget, you will probably be able to purchase only warm beer or soda from the roadside vendors, neither of which is appealing on a hot day. You may want to bring food, too. If you purchase vegetables or fruit while traveling, wash them with the bottled water that you brought from Yerevan.

## HALF-DAY TRIPS FROM YEREVAN

**Echmiadzin** (originally established in AD 301) is the seat of the Armenian Church, and is the holiest of religious sites in Armenia. The complex consists of several buildings, including the main cathedral on the church campus, and two other churches nearby. There have been several modifications and additions to the main cathedral, including a major reconstruction in the fifth century AD. The Manukian Museum at the main cathedral contains the **Treasures of Echmiadzin**, and the campus is filled with ancient *khatchkars* and religious monuments. The old pagan altar, over which the cathedral was built, can be viewed by entering a small room at the rear of the building.

Off campus, but nearby, are the two churches of **St. Gayane** and **St. Hripsime**, which were each built in the seventh century. **Zvartnots Cathedral** is located midway along the Echmiadzin roadway and can be visited during the same trip. The

R. Kurkjian                                                              St. Gayane, Echmiadzin

architecture of Zvartnots is unique among Armenian churches, but an earthquake leveled it in the tenth century. The site is now a ruin of pillars, but a reconstructed model is on display at the State Museum of Armenian History.

*Travel time from Yerevan to Echmiadzin and Zvartnots is about 30 minutes. Don't take the slow #111 bus. Instead, hire a private driver for the entire trip, for about $15 to $20 for one half day. From Yerevan, drive west past the airport on Admiral Isakov Street.*

Roughly 30 km west of Echmiadzin, near the town of Hoktemberian, is the battle monument of **Sardarapat**. A monument and an archaeological and folk art museum mark the location of what is certainly Armenia's most significant military victory of the modern era. In 1918, Kemalist Turkish forces internationalized the Genocide by invading the Armenian regions of what was then part of the Russian Empire. The Turks were turned back at Sardarapat, however, and the Armenian nation survived. It is unlikely that the current Armenian republic would exist if this battle had been lost. The stone statues of two massive winged lions flank a bell tower. Relics from the battle are among the items at the nearby museum.

*Travel time from Echmiadzin is about 30 minutes. To reach Sardarapat, travel west through Armavir and Noravan, and then south to Hoktemberian. Combine this trip with a visit to Echmiadzin.*

**Geghard Monastery** is a fascinating complex of buildings that are built into the side of a mountain. The grounds are home to several magnificent *khatchkars*, and there is frequently a trio of musicians performing folk music in the parking lot, which adds to the magical ambience of this wonderful site. **Garni Temple** is located just off the roadway before you reach Geghard, and you should stop here as part of your excursion. The temple was built in the first century AD by an Armenian king, and is now the site of the oldest known *khatchkar* extant, dating from AD 879. There are still many ancient *khatchkars* at the site, as well as the tile ruins of the King's bathhouse. Earthquakes throughout history have destroyed the temple. The building was reconstructed in 1975.

The temple overlooks a deep canyon, which is known as **Garni Gorge**. This canyon is popular with hikers and it provides a potential access point to the **Khosrov Preserve**, which is home to many endangered plants and animals. Access is officially prohibited, but hikers are sometimes allowed to pass. A cobblestone and gravel road leads down to the gorge from a point not far from the temple. Spectacular basalt columns stretch upward from the canyon floor. There is no admission fee to Geghard, but foreign visitors to Garni are charged 200 dram (about fifty cents). Professional photographers are asked for 2,000 dram (about $5). On your return trip to Yerevan, stop at **Azat Reservoir** if there's time. The lake is west of the main road (on the left if you are returning to Yerevan from the Garni temple) and is a great setting for a picnic. You won't see the lake from the roadway, but there's a narrow paved road that will take you right up to its shores.

*Travel time from Yerevan to Geghard and Garni is about 45 minutes. Hire a private driver for about $20 for the entire half-day trip. If you plan to hike in the gorge, add several hours to the trip, and an extra fee for the driver, who will wait for you.*

**Khor Virap Monastery** is a shrine to Armenian Christianity. The monastery is surrounded by tall walls, and the gates are closed each day at 5 pm, but this shouldn't deter you from visiting at sunset, when the orange glow of the sun can make this one of the most spectacular sights in the country. The church complex was built atop the pit where St. Gregory the Illuminator had been imprisoned, on the Ararat plain near the Arax River. This river forms the international boundary between Armenia and Turkey, so you won't be permitted to approach its shallow banks.

*Khor Virap*                                           M. Karanian

R. Kurkjian                                                                                    Ashtarak

Ararat is the mountain that snagged the bottom of Noah's ark, and it is the spiritual heart of Armenia. The Armenians make a legendary claim that they are descendants of Noah and so Ararat is central to Armenian self-identity. The mountain is depicted on Armenian currency, and its peaks adorn the republic's coat of arms. Ararat is the tallest mountain of historic Armenia, at 5,165 meters, and it soars in the national consciousness as well. It cannot be claimed as the tallest mountain in the modern Republic of Armenia, however. Mt. Ararat lies just outside its border. Khor Virap is as close as you can get to this mountain without going to Turkey, so enjoy the view.

This is also the heart of Armenia's **Ararat Valley**, which is reputed to be the hottest and driest place in the country, so if you visit during the summer this is an extra incentive to go at sunset, after the hottest part of the day has gone. Go early in the morning if you want to walk inside the compound. The hot weather is great for the watermelons that are grown here, which farmers sell on the roadside in August and September. If you hesitate about a purchase, the farmer will cut out a core of the fruit to show you how fresh it is! There's a military base nearby, and several watchtowers throughout the valley, which are manned by Russian soldiers. Don't point your camera at them. Photography of the soldiers or of the military stations is forbidden. There was no admission fee to the monastery in 2000, but you might be asked for 100 dram (twenty cents) for parking.

*Travel time from Yerevan to Khor Virap and the Ararat Valley is about one hour. Hire a driver for about $20 for a stay lasting a couple of hours.*

Visits to **Mt. Aragats** (elevation 4,090 meters) are especially rewarding during the summer, when temperatures here can be ten degrees cooler (Celsius) than in Yerevan. This is Armenia's tallest mountain, and non-professionals can climb most of it in four or five hours, after first driving to the end of the mountain access road. Hiking shoes and stamina are the only essential gear. Access roads to the mountain are located on both the west and east sides. There's snow cover here year-round, so

*Mt. Aragats*                                                                 *M. Karanian*

the best time to visit is in the summer. The air is thin, so go slowly. To reach **Amberd Fortress**, which is located near the slopes of Aragats at roughly 2,300 meters, take the east road, which is also the road that leads to Spitak and take the left turnoff to the mountain. A directional arrow is spray-painted on the asphalt road. The fort and the adjoining church were built in the eleventh century, and offer magnificent vistas. There's an ancient graveyard just a five minute walk from here.

*Travel time from Yerevan to Amberd, and the rest of the way to Aragats, is about ninety minutes because of all the switchbacks. Hire a driver for between $20 and $30 for the half day. If you plan to hike at Aragats, plan to spend the entire day there.*

The town of **Ashtarak** is just 20 km north of Yerevan, and is worth a separate visit for its ancient monuments. From the bridge that crosses the Kasakh River, and which leads to the town, you can see three of the town's churches all at once. The most famous is the **Karmravor Church**, which was built in the seventh century.

*Travel time from Yerevan to Ashtarak is about thirty minutes. Hire a driver for about $20 for the half day, or combine this visit with stops at Aragats, Amberd and Saghmosavank.*

Along the roadway that leads from Yerevan to Spitak, in the Ashtarak region, there are a trio of sites that can be visited in one half day. **Saghmosavank** stands atop the gorge of the Kasakh River, and is a dramatic example of thirteenth century architecture. This is the most popular of the three sites. **Caving and hiking** opportunities are here, too. Just a few kilometers closer to Yerevan is **Tegherivank**, also from the thirteenth century. And closest to Yerevan on the Yerevan-to-Spitak road is **Mughni**, from the fourteenth century.

*Travel time from Yerevan to Saghmosavank is about 45 minutes. Hire a driver for about $20 for the half day. For a full day of touring, combine visits to these churches with a stop at Amberd and Aragats.*

## FULL-DAY TRIPS FROM YEREVAN

**Gyumri** (population 225,000) is Armenia's second-largest city, and it is notorious these days as the biggest city in the earthquake zone, so-called for the huge quake that struck there on December 7, 1988. There has been some reconstruction, but as of 2000 many people were still living in the metal shipping containers (*domiks*) that were converted to temporary housing more than ten years ago. There's also an old Russian fortress in Gyumri, and a statue of **Mother Armenia**.

Thirty minutes away by car, there's a great lookout point from which you can see across the Armenian-Turkish border to the ancient Armenian capital of **Ani**. To get close enough to see anything, you'll need permission from the soldiers on duty there. Drive west out of the city, and then south along the main roadway just inside the Armenia-Turkey border.

Don't be in such a big rush to zip up to Gyumri, though. There are several sites south of Gyumri that are worth stopping for along the way. From Yerevan, heading north along the roadway that leads from Yerevan to Gyumri, there are several ancient sites, including a twelfth century *khatchkar* that is believed to be the biggest ever made, and a thirteenth century caravansary. The *khatchkar* dates from AD 1195, and you'll see it just off the main road shortly before the turnoff to the village of Kosh. The caravansary is farther north on the left side of the main road, near the village of Aruch. A short detour to the town of **Talin** yields a trio of ancient religious sites, including the seventh century church of St. Astvatsatsin. To get there, take the turnoff from the main road toward Talin, and then turn right onto the second intersecting road.

*Travel time from Yerevan to Gyumri is about ninety minutes, and about two hours to the Ani lookout. Stop at Talin on the way north to Gyumri, or bypass Gyumri completely and visit the Ani lookout, instead. Hire a driver for about $40 for this full day excursion. A bus departs daily each morning from Kilikia Central Bus Station.*

**Spitak** was completely leveled in the earthquake of 1988, because of its proximity to the earthquake's epicenter. Many of the town's residents still live in metal shipping containers, which were intended as temporary housing, but much of the town has been rebuilt, especially during the past couple of years. At the approach to Spitak, there's a whimsical church on the left side of the road that looks every bit like a traditional Armenian church, except that it is made from sheet metal. This non-traditional material was used so that the church could be quickly erected to accommodate the many funerals that were held after the quake. You've got to stop and take a closer look at this one.

From Spitak, the roads split off to **Vanadzor** to the east, Gyumri to the west, and **Stepanavan** to the north. The road to Stepanavan passes through a newly re-constructed tunnel. Traveling through this tunnel is like traveling into a different world. On the southern side, the landscape is brown and stark. Beyond the tunnel, the road is shaded by lush woodland, and the climate is more temperate because of all the vegetation. This roadway through Stepanavan offers the most direct route to Tbilisi, Georgia. The roadway through Vanadzor is longer, but offers more sightseeing opportunities.

*Travel time to Spitak and Vanadzor from Yerevan is about seventy minutes and ninety minutes, respectively. Travel time to Stepanavan is about three hours. Hire a driver for about $40 to Spitak or Vanadzor, and about $50 to Stepanavan. On the left side of the road, just before reaching Stepanavan, there's a small motel where you can rent a comfortable room for about $8 for each person, with breakfast.*

**Tsaghkadzor** was popular as a ski resort during the Soviet era, but there haven't been many skiers in the past decade. There's a chair lift that operates, however, and there are still some trails that you can ski down, if you provide your own skis and equipment. The region today is popular in the fall because of the colorful foliage, and as a resort for picnickers and hikers throughout the year. **Kecharis Monastery** is located near the Writer's Union House, which is operated as a hotel. To get there from Yerevan, travel on the Yerevan-to-Sevan roadway for about 50 km. There's a right hand turn off for Tsaghkadzor that loops under the main roadway, just before you reach Sevan.

*Travel time to Tsaghkadzor from Yerevan is about forty-five minutes. Hire a driver for about $30. Stop here on the way to Sevan, or make a separate full day trip to see the fall foliage.*

## Places to Stay

Overnight lodging is available in Gyumri at the modern "**Gastehaus Berlin**" (Tel. 2-31-48) for about $50. Located at 25 Haghtanaki Street near the center of the city. In the center of town, **Hotel Isuz** offers eight double rooms and four suites in a large and modern facility. There are also conference rooms and several shops. Single $60; Deluxe suite $100. (Tel. 3-33-99; Fax 3-99-93). Located at 1/5 Garegin Njdeh Ave. When calling from outside Gyumri, be sure to use the city code (41) before entering the local phone number. In Tsaghkadzor, lodging is available at the Writer's Union House for about $30 per night. Rooms have running hot water (Tel. 5-25-39; 5-25-32).

*Ruins at Stepanavan*                                              *M. Karanian*

# LONGER TRIPS

## LAKE SEVAN

You can easily visit **Lake Sevan** in one day, but it deserves more. Sevan is a great spot for a two-day, overnight excursion, especially for travelers who are touring as a family, because it offers outdoor recreational activities, in addition to traditional sightseeing. You can swim for free at any of a string of beaches located along the northwestern shore. The best and most **secluded beaches** are the ones that you cannot see from the road. These are also the beaches that aren't listed in any of the tourist brochures. To reach them from Yerevan, take the right hand turn-off near the village of Sevan, which is located at the northwestern shore of the lake. You'll see the turn at roughly the same time that the lake comes into view.

*Courtesy of the Birds of Armenia Project, American University of Armenia, Oakland, CA, 1999*

At the northern shore near the town of Sevan, there are a couple of privately operated beaches that offer modest amenities such as umbrellas, chairs and cafes. **Paddleboats** and **rowboats** are available for rental by the hour. There's usually a $5 charge for parking. Regardless of which beach you select, the water is clear and cold, and in the summer it acquires a turquoise hue that can fool you into thinking you're in the Greek Isles. To charter a catamaran **sailboat** with a captain by the hour or by the day, check with the manager of the Blue Sevan Motel, or with one of their authorized travel agents, which are all listed below in Places to Stay. There were no bicycle rentals available at the lake when we checked in 2000.

There are several *khorovats* (barbecue) stands along this road where you can purchase a meal of kebob and roasted vegetables. We have found that they often don't have bread or cold drinks, so treat these places as a supplement to the provisions that you bring from Yerevan. Be sure to request well-cooked meat.

If you hire a private driver, you can travel around the entire lake in one full day. The spectacular ecology of the region would justify doing it in two days. But unless you're a birder or an environmental scientist, most of the compelling attractions are on the west shore road, stretching roughly from the northern town of Sevan, and as far south as Noraduz.

From the road near the town of Sevan you can see the **Sevan Monastery**, **Sevanavank**. This religious site is located on a peninsula that had been an island until only a half century ago, before agricultural and urban use drained away massive amounts of Sevan's water. Of greatest interest are two ninth century churches, **Arakelots** and **Astvatsatsin**, at the top of a long flight of stairs. They have both been extensively renovated during the past few years. The foundation ruins of a third ancient church are located just a few yards away, and khatchkars are plentiful, too. From this site you'll have a wonderful view of the lake and the distant mountains. Admission is free, but there's usually someone collecting money at the parking lot, typically about 100 dram (20 cents).

Birders will want to stop near **Gull Island**, located a few kilometers south of the town of Sevan, along the west shore road. The seagulls that gather here are joined by dozens of other bird species. Farther south in **Kamo**, which has been renamed **Gavar**, the Tenth Century monastery **Hairavank** is perched atop a cliff at the water's edge. **Noraduz**, which is famous for its cemetery of thousands of *khatchkars*, is nearby.

*Travel time by car from Yerevan to Sevanavank and Gull Island is about one hour, and about ninety minutes to Gavar (Kamo). Hire a driver for roughly $30 for a half day or $40 for a full day. A one-way drop off probably won't save money. Travel by van every Saturday and Sunday morning during the summer. Fare is 900 dram (about $2). The vans line up along the perimeter of the park on the corner of Sayat Nova Ave. and Moskovian Street, near the Manhattan City Bar. Departure times are when all the seats in a particular van are filled, and generally start around 10 am and conclude by noon.*

*M. Karanian*                                   *Hairvank Churchyard*

## Places to Stay

Hotels in the Sevan Region do not customarily take reservations by telephone. You can make a reservation in person, but this isn't always practical for a foreign tourist, who may only make one trip to the region. Your options are to make a booking through a Yerevan travel agent, to drive up in advance of your planned stay to book a room, or to just be flexible and go there early in the day to look for a room, with the expectation that you'll stay if you find one, or go back to Yerevan if you cannot. As with any trip in the Armenian countryside, you will need to be flexible in order to have a pleasant journey.

**Sevan Two Motel** has balconies overlooking the lake, and clean rooms in two large buildings. Most of the 101 rooms have hot water, but some don't get any. Reservations advised in August. Cafeteria food for an additional $5 daily. Single $15; Double $25. Located on the water near Sevanavank monastery.

The **Hotel** with no name is a grand Soviet era building with marginally better accommodations. Hot water and televisions in all rooms, restaurant and bar on site. A final choice if the other lodges are full. Single $30; Suite $40. Located on the northern shore, next to several construction projects that were halted about a decade ago.

**Blue Sevan** is the best the lake has to offer. A large campground featuring 10 cottages and a building with 37 rooms. Hot water in all rooms, private baths in the main building, shared showers for the cottages. Cafeteria open during the summer. Per person: $12- $18. Hidden location. After passing the Soviet-era "Hotel," access through a metal gate (painted bright blue in 2000) that leads to a long drive down to the beach. Reservations can be made from Yerevan by calling **Delta Armenia Travel Agency**, 4 Kievian Street, near Baghramian (Tel. 56-60-99; 22-56-54) or **Elitar Agency**, 17 Terian Street (Tel. 54-33-11).

The **Avan Marak Tsapatagh**, a 34-room hotel and resort complex, was scheduled to open in the summer of 2002. Plans for this beachfront facility include a restau-

*Lake Sevan*          *R. Kurkjian*

rant and a craft center that will support local artisans. The lodge will be located in Tsapatagh village, on the shores of Lake Sevan. Anticipated room rates: Single $40; Double $70. (E-mail: tufhosp@arminco.com) (www.tufenkian.am).

## DILIJAN

Armenians call this forested region in the northwest their Little Switzerland. The wooden buildings and porches you'll see here are a rare sight in Armenia. The moist and cool climate makes this a great retreat from the summer heat of Yerevan, and the region was popular among vacationers during the Soviet era. The Dilijan region is also famous for its **mineral water**, which is bottled and sold as a health tonic. The bottling plant is located about 3 km outside town on the road that leads to Vanadzor. You'll also find an interesting Russian village, with an onion-domed wood-frame church, along this route between Dilijan and Vanadzor.

The greatest regional attractions are the monasteries of **Haghardzin** and **Goshavank**, which were built in the Middle Ages. Haghardzin is located east of Dilijan, and you can reach it by traveling on the main road toward the town of Ijevan. The monastery complex consists of three churches and a dining hall. The oldest of the churches, St. Gregory, was built in the tenth century. The other churches, St. Stepanos and St. Astvatsatsin, as well as the refectory, date back to the thirteenth century.

Goshavank's complex consists of three churches, as well as a large reading hall. The buildings were constructed in the late twelfth and early thirteenth centuries. The monastery itself was founded in 1188 and it formed a significant cultural center during the Middle Ages.

For a restful picnic spot, try the small lake known as **Parz Lich**. The English translation of the name is Clear Lake, which seems to be a misnomer for the greenish-hued water. There's no swimming at this lake, but the forested environs make it a pleasant stop and you may be able to rent a rowboat. Hiking and mountain bicycling are also

popular in Dilijan, especially at the **Dilijan Nature Reserve**. The most direct travel route to Dilijan from Yerevan is the Yerevan-to-Sevan road north through the Sevan Pass, which is the passage between the mountains. Along this roadway you'll also find a village populated by ethnic Russians who were relocated here during the Stalin era.

*Travel time by car from the north shore of Lake Sevan is less than one hour. From Yerevan, allow two hours.*

## Places to Stay

**Hotel Dilijan**, Soviet era accommodations. Singles from $2-$10. Prominently located near the town center. **Cinematographers' Union House**, cottages and private rooms with hot water. Double $20; Cottage $50. Located in vicinity of Hotel Dilijan. Restaurant open during the Summer. **Sounk Motel**, clean and private rooms with hot water, located on a veranda above the inn's restaurant. Single $10. Located in Dilijan on the main road that leads to Ijevan.

## ALAVERDI – LORI REGION

The lush and remote region of **Lori** in the north is home to three of the most magical and beautiful monasteries of Armenia: **Sanahin**, **Haghpat** and **Odzun**. Any one of them alone would be worth the trip. Because of their proximity to each other in the town of **Alaverdi**, however, it is an easy matter to visit all three during one outing. The Sanahin and Haghpat Monasteries are located on wooded mountainsides in Alaverdi. Odzun is nearby, as well, and is perched on a large table of flatland atop a gorge.

Sanahin was founded in AD 966 and its surviving complex today consists of a bell tower, library, and a pair of churches. The bell tower dates back to 1211 and is said to be the oldest of its kind in Armenia. Many more buildings, including libraries and dwellings, have formed part of the monastery campus in the past. Haghpat was built at roughly the same time and it shares many architectural elements with Sanahin. This fortified monastery is only about two miles away, and is built at the top of the Debed River Gorge. Haghpat served as a major literary and cultural center during the Middle Ages.

The oldest of the trio of monasteries is Odzun, which was built in the early eighth century. This complex also sits atop the Debed River Gorge, where it could be defended against invaders. Just a few meters from the main church is a sixth century funeral monument on which is engraved scenes that depict the early spread of Christianity.

There's an **ancient bridge**, built in 1192, that spans the Debed River and that you will see on your way to Sanahin. It had been open to motor vehicles as recently as the 1970s, but it is now closed and cars are directed over a modern bridge. There are also **copper** mines along the Debed River in Alaverdi which both spurred the town's growth and also spoiled some of its appearance. The mines are operating at low capacity today and scientists are monitoring their effects upon local water resources.

West of Alaverdi, near the town of Stepanavan, the ruins of the fortress of Lori are the highlight of the town of **Lori Berd**. The fort dates back to the tenth century. Although this area is within the geographic region of Lori, the roadways make it more convenient to visit Stepanavan as part of a trip north past Spitak.

You can make it to Alaverdi and back to Yerevan in one tiring day if you start early. Start from Dilijan or Sevan to save time, or consider staying overnight. Lodging

*Regional Guide*

*Photograph: Winter in the Lake Sevan region, R. Kurkjian*

options in Alaverdi are few, so you will need to be flexible, although a modern lodge is scheduled to open there in 2002.

*Travel time to Alaverdi from Yerevan is at least four hours, depending upon road conditions.*

## Places to Stay

Construction is underway on the **Avan Spa Dzoraget**, a modern 34-room hotel in the Alaverdi area, near the Sanahin Monastery. When this lodge opens in late 2002 it will feature such amenities as a swimming pool, restaurant and conference center. Until it opens, however, there's really nothing we can recommend nearby except for some family-operated rooming houses that seem to come and go over the years.

*Travel time from Yerevan is at least four hours, depending upon road conditions.*

# ZANGEZUR

## THE TOP OF THE PANHANDLE

To reach the panhandle of Armenia from Yerevan, you must travel through the Ararat Valley, and then make an abrupt left turn (east) just before you approach the **Nakhijevan**-Armenia border. Nakhijevan's population once had a plurality of Armenians, but today it is a non-contiguous administrative unit of Azerbaijan, and the Armenians have all disappeared. The border is closed, and there's no risk that you can accidentally stray too close, thanks to a barricade set up by the Armenians. Do not attempt to reach the panhandle by the alternate route from Lake Sevan and through the **Vayots Dzor Pass**. This unpleasant shortcut will add at least five hours of driving time on rough dirt roads.

On the right (west) side of the road, a couple of kilometers before you reach the Nakhijevan border, there are several fish farms where trout are produced. You'll see fish for sale at the roadside here, too. The region around these fish farms are great birding locations. The first town you reach in the panhandle is **Areni**, which gives its name to the famous Armenian wine. Grapes are grown throughout this region, and if you visit in October, you may be able to see the winemaking process here or in the nearby towns of **Getap** and **Arpi**.

There's only one north-south roadway in Armenia, so it's almost impossible to get lost in the panhandle. It is also likely that your vehicle will be stopped, at least briefly, at one of the military checkpoints along this road. The checkpoints are startling to many Western tourists, but they are as routine to the locals as tollbooths are to Americans.

Immediately after passing Areni, there's a turnoff on the right side of the main road which leads to a stunning bedrock canyon and the **Noravank Monastery**. This ancient monastery's name has renewed meaning now that the complex has been completely rebuilt. The English translation of Noravank is "new monastery." Two flights of narrow steps lead to the main hall of **Astvatsatsin Church** and there are several *khatchkars* in the churchyard. From the church you'll have a panoramic view of the rocky yet verdant setting. Another interesting site in the area is the ruin of the Tsakhatskar Monastery, parts of which date back to the tenth century.

There are several caverns in the Vayots Dzor region, just outside the town of **Yeghegnadzor** with dramatic stalactite and stalagmite formations. Most of these areas

*Photograph: Yeghegnadzor canyon, R. Kurkjian*

are dangerous, however, even for experienced cavers. They are also environmentally sensitive. We urge you to avoid them. Just outside town you'll see Armenia's version of a truck stop. There are a dozen or so vendors selling farm produce, sandwiches, coffee and drinks. If you didn't pack a lunch from home, you may be able to find something here.

Just after passing the town of Vayk, there's a left turnoff for **Jermuk**. This is the site of the mineral springs that produce the Jermuk water that is popular throughout the country. Jermuk is a great break on a longer journey. It is also a fine destination for hiking or for recreation near the waterfall along Jermuk's Arpa River. The Soviet-era health spas in the area (called sanatoriums), are unappealing. The natural environment, however, is breathtaking, and worth a visit. The detour takes about 30 minutes. Before reaching **Sisian** you pass the **Spandarian Reservoir**, a man-made lake that serves the region's hydropower needs. Farther south near Shaki, the famous **Shaki Waterfall** is an interesting diversion. The regional highlight here, however, is at Sisian. Here you'll find **Zorakar**, a circular arrangement of stones that is believed to be a celestial observatory. The site is similar to England's Stonehenge, but Armenia's is from the Bronze Age, making it much older. To reach the site directly from the main road, turn right at the second of the two Sisian turnoffs and travel less than one half kilometer. The site is in a desolate field on the right. There's a military checkpoint on the main road nearby.

*Travel time from Yerevan to Sisian is roughly four hours, if you drive without stopping at Jermuk or any of the other interesting sights. If you are continuing south, you may want to spend the night here. Sisian is the last place with good lodgings until you reach Karabagh, and we strongly recommend that you avoid driving to Karabagh after dark because of the unlighted and winding mountain roads, which are often foggy in winter.*

## Place to Stay

**Sisian's Dina Hotel** was built in 1936, but the new management has made this a comfortable and clean place to stay. Each of the 31 rooms has 24-hour hot water, telephone, television, and a pair of twin beds in each room. $3 Single; $6 Deluxe. 35 Sisakan Street (Tel. 50-34-71).

# ZANGEZUR

# THE MIDDLE OF THE PANHANDLE

**Tatev Monastery** looms high above the town of the same name. You'll see the complex long before you reach it along winding dirt roads. The monastery was originally built in the ninth century, and it served for many years as a regional center and as a fortress against foreign invasion. St. Gregory of Tatev (1346-1409), one of the staunchest defenders of the Armenian Church, is buried here, and his grave is a pilgrimage destination for Armenians. An earthquake ruined the monastery in 1932, and a major renovation has been underway for the past several years. One of the many interesting monuments at Tatev is a 25-foot-tall octagonal pillar with an engraved khatchkar at the top. This uncommon structure, named Gavazan, was built in AD 904. Shortly afterward, in AD 930, the interior walls of the main church of Bogos and Bedros were decorated with frescoes, but the imagery is now almost totally lost. There are many other ancient monuments and examples of unique or uncommon buildings at Tatev, making this one of the most admired and cherished architectural sites in Armenia. At its zenith, more than 600 monks studied and prayed at Tatev, making this one of the nation's most significant religious sites, as well.

*Photograph: Zorakar, M. Karanian*

Near Tatev there's a natural rock formation known as **Devil's Bridge**, and a hot spring, either of which would make good stop-off points on your way to the monastery.

*To get to Tatev: traveling south from Yerevan, there's a right turnoff before reaching Goris, near a police checkpoint. This is not a quick detour. Travel time from Goris is about two hours on poor roads. There is no lodging at Tatev, so allow enough time to return to Goris before dark.*

**Goris** is a quaint town completely surrounded by mountains, and located along the main north-south highway. More interesting than the town, however, are the caves and exotic rock formations at nearby **Khundzoresk**. Many of the caves are today used as barns for farm animals. Several centuries ago people occupied them. This is a fabulous place to stop and spend a couple of hours hiking or picnicking. Traveling south from Yerevan, go about two kilometers past Goris to a turnoff on the right side. Travel down this road for less than two kilometers and turn right again.

*Travel time from Yerevan to Goris without stopping is about five hours. From Sisian, the drive is about one hour. Travel time from Tatev to Goris is about two hours. Travel time from Goris to Khundzoresk is about fifteen minutes.*

## Place to Stay

**Goris Hotel** is a rundown Soviet era hotel located at the far end of Goris. If you want water in your room you'll have to carry it up in a pail. This is a dreary spot to be avoided except in an emergency. Foreigners pay about $20 for a bed in a room, which is roughly ten times what travelers with Armenian passports pay. This two-tiered pricing is a carry-over from Soviet days, too.

# ZANGEZUR

# THE BOTTOM OF THE PANHANDLE

After reaching Goris, you will have two travel options. You can either travel east to Karabagh, by way of the Goris to Stepanakert highway, or you can continue south to the Iranian border. Either destination will add two days to your journey from Goris, or three days from Yerevan. For full details on traveling to Karabagh, see the section on Karabagh elsewhere in this book.

If you opt for the southern route to the Iranian border, you will first pass through the Armenian town of **Kapan**. This was a strategic military location during the Soviet era, and it was also the site of many mining operations. Today the mines are closed, and there are no big attractions for tourists. The mountainous roads make the 65 km journey from Goris seem much longer. Snow and ice obstructed some of the mountain passes as early as October during our visits. There's an old Soviet hotel in town which is much more comfortable than the one in Goris, which makes Kapan a better overnight stop if you're passing through.

**Meghri** is the final Armenian town before reaching Iran. The climate here is subtropical, and it is common to see pomegranates and figs growing on trees along the roads. There are several ancient sites here, including an old fortress, but for most travelers, Meghri is merely the Armenian outpost on the way to Iran. The Armenia-Iran border is open, and relations between the two countries are friendly, making this a good access point to Iran. Visas are required for transit into Iran, and you can apply for one at the Iranian Embassy in Yerevan. Refer to the *Essentials* chapter of this guide for contact information.

*Travel time from Yerevan to Meghri without stopping is about ten hours. Travel time from Goris is about five hours. Travel time from Goris to Kapan is about two hours, and from Kapan to Meghri it is about three hours. We recommend that you stay overnight in Kapan, and that you avoid traveling after dark, because of the poor road conditions.*

## Places to Stay

**Hotel Lernagordz** in Kapan is a Soviet era hotel, but it is much more comfortable than many, and we recommend it above anything else in the region, including the hotel in Goris. Foreigners can expect to pay $20 each. Located in the center of Kapan. There's a hotel in Meghri, as well, but accomodations are poor.

## SUGGESTED ITINERARIES

### One Day

Echmiadzin's main cathedral in the morning, the Matenadaran at mid-day, and Khor Virap at sunset. After sunset, Republic Square in Yerevan.

### Two or Three Days

Drive to Khor Virap Monastery in the Ararat Valley at sunrise. In central Yerevan, spend mid-day at Republic Square, Katoghike Church, and the Matenadaran. Then add Zvartnots, and the three main churches of Echmiadzin. Drive to the Genocide Memorial at sunset. On the second day, add a trek out to Geghard and Garni, with stops in the countryside. For active travelers, explore Azat Reservoir, or the Garni Gorge. On the third day, add a trip to Lake Sevan and the monasteries there, as well as Noraduz.

### One Week to Ten Days

Combine a trek to Noravank with your visit to Khor Virap. On days four and five, see Amberd Fortress, Mt. Aragats, the Karmravor Church in Ashtarak, and the Saghmosavank monastery. Spend an extra day in Yerevan on the weekend, and visit the *Vernissage* (arts market) and one of the regular *shuka* markets. On days seven and eight add a long journey to the Alaverdi-Lori region, and an easier day trip to Tsaghkadzor. Visit Dilijan last, if you have time and energy.

### Two or Three Weeks

Add a daylong excursion to Gyumri, with a stop in Talin along the way. Travel down into the Zangezur panhandle, and to Stepanakert, for a stay of at least one night, ideally two or three. On the return to Yerevan, stop at Khundzoresk and at Zorakar. Spend an overnight in Sisian if necessary. Add a second day at Lake Sevan and Dilijan.

### More than Three Weeks

Add an excursion all the way south to Meghri, the small Armenian town near the Iranian border. Plan to spend several days winding your way south to Meghri from Yerevan, with extended stops at Jermuk and Tatev along the way. On the return trek northward, detour to Karabagh, with a stay of several nights—long enough to visit the remote Dadivank Monastery and the beautiful Sarsang Reservoir.

Regional Guide

In a land with a bounty of stones, it is not surprising that artisans and craftsmen would use this medium to express their talents.

This artistic expression found its voice, beginning early in the fourth century AD, in the Christian exaltation of the cross. Winged crosses made from large stones, were erected to replace some of the earliest wooden crosses of the era. The earliest of these winged crosses have been discovered at the ancient Armenian capital of Dvin.

From these early prototypes, the Armenians developed the *khatchkar*—an art form of engraved stone crosses that is unique to their culture. These khatchkars first became a national art form in the ninth and tenth centuries, and the oldest of them is believed to be one that was erected in AD 879 by the wife of an Armenian king. Ironically, or perhaps intentionally, the chosen site was in Garni, next to a pagan temple that had been built during Armenia's pre-Christian era.

These early stone crosses were probably commissioned in order to secure salvation of the soul. But by the twelfth and thirteenth centuries, they were also erected to commemorate historic events such as military battles or the construction of a monastery. Others, especially those that are set into the walls of churches, may honor individuals who made significant contributions to that church. Khatchkars were also used as tombstones. Three of these, dating back to AD 1211, are at the Haghpat Monastery in northern Armenia.

Some of the artisans who carved these stones were master architects who also constructed many fine churches. Today, experts acclaim their engravings from the medieval era as the finest the Armenians created. Some of these thirteenth century masterpieces are found at the monastery of Geghard, which is located about 50 km outside Yerevan, and at Goshavank, which is a bit more remote from the capital.

Foreign invasions disrupted the artistic development of khatchkars in the fourteenth century, but there was eventually a limited revival. From the sixteenth through eighteenth centuries, khatchkars were mostly used as tombstones. Thousands were created during this time, and there are hundreds of examples at the cemeteries of Noraduz and Jugha. Noraduz is located about 30 km south of the town of Sevan, on the western shore of Lake Sevan. Jugha is located in Nakhijevan. Art experts say the engravings from the Middle Ages, however, represent the zenith of this art form.

## LONG WEEKENDS

## THE REPUBLIC OF GEORGIA

Georgia, another of the former Soviet Republics, is located across Armenia's north-ern border. You should allow at least three days for travel if you plan to visit as part of your Armenia trip. Many ethnic groups live there, usually in disparate regions, with varying degrees of autonomy from the country's central leadership. Among these peoples is a community of roughly 500,000 ethnic Armenians that is con-centrated in Tbilisi, Javakh, and Abkhazia.

The tourism infrastructure of Georgia is perhaps the best in the Caucasus. The Georgian capital city, Tbilisi, draws far more tourists than any location in Armenia. Many parts of the country are dangerous, however, because of civil unrest or sepa-ratist fighting. Travelers should avoid traveling north of Tbilisi.

The national language is Georgian, which has its own unique alphabet, as does Armenian. At a glance, the Georgian alphabet looks similar to the Armenian one. It should. Mesrop Mashtots created them both. Russian is also spoken, but this lan-guage, and the country from which it originates, are currently in disfavor among Georgians. English is not widely spoken. Armenian is fairly common in Tbilisi, however, and it is ubiquitous in and around Akhalkalak, in the Javakh region west of the capital.

Travelers going to Georgia need a visa, which is available from the **Georgian Embassy**. In Yerevan: 42 Arami Street (Tel. 56-13-67; 58-55-11). In Washington, DC: 1511 K Street, NW (Tel. 202-393-6060; Internet: www.georgiaemb.org). The fee for a one-week visa is $40. If this is a side trip, and you plan to return to Armenia, you will need a multiple entry visa from Armenia. Visas typically permit only one entry, so be sure to plan ahead. If you forget, don't fret. There's an Armenian embassy in Tbilisi where you can get a new visa.

### The Armenian-Populated Areas

**Tbilisi** is home to most of Georgia's Armenians, and they are concentrated in the **Avlabari** district, which is close to the center of town. Avlabari can be easily reached by walking across the Metekhi Bridge, near the Metekhi Church, or by taking the metro to the Avlabari Square station. The church of **Echmiadzin**, which bears the same name as the seat of the Armenian church in Armenia, and which was built in 1804, stands tall at the west end of the district, near the bridge. You'll see it to the right when you walk out of the metro station. There's an Armenian theater at the other side of the square, where there are concerts and dance performances through-out the year, except during August. At the other end of the bridge, near Gorgasali Square, is the church of **St. Gregory**, or Surb Gevorg, which was built in AD 1251.

Travel time to Tbilisi from Yerevan by private car is about five or six hours. The roadway through the Armenian town of **Stepanavan** is a bit faster, but the route through Alaverdi in Armenia offers an opportunity to stop and see some of

*Photograph on previous page: Katchkar at Echmiadzin, R. Kurkjian*

Armenia's most beautiful monasteries along the way. Each route passes through the Georgian town of Marneuli, which is populated almost entirely by ethnic Azeris. We advise against stopping in this town if your car has Armenian license plates. Bus schedules from Yerevan are listed in the Armenia chapter under international travel.

**Akhalkalak** is located in the remote **Javakh** region west of Tbilisi, and is home to roughly 30,000 ethnic Armenians. Commentators have pointed to this region as Georgia's next hot spot of ethnic problems, but their predictions have so far proven to be more alarmist than accurate. The greatest concern of most of the people that we have spoken to here appears to be economic, and not political. Armenians originally settled here as refugees from the Ottoman Empire in 1828, after Russia re-established control of the area. The oldest surviving Armenian church here is **Surb Sargis**, which was built in 1830 in the village of Deeleeskah, located just about 5 km from Akhalkalak. **Surb Khatch** was built in the center of town in 1856, and was undergoing extensive repairs in 2000. Perhaps the highlight of the region, however, is the dramatically located **Akhalkalak Fortress**, just outside town.

To reach this area by private car, drive north from Yerevan through the Armenian city of Gyumri. The road in Armenia from Gyumri to the Armenian-Georgian border is in excellent condition, and traveling to the border from Yerevan takes only about two hours. The roads deteriorate at the border, however. Travel time for the rest of the journey within Georgia is at least five hours, on dirt and gravel. Bus schedules from Yerevan are listed in the Armenia chapter under international travel.

There is also a significant Armenian community in **Abkhazia**, but travelers absolutely must avoid this region. The ethnic Abkhazians have been fighting a separatist war against Georgia for the past decade, and the region is militarized and especially dangerous to Westerners, who are sometimes seized as hostages by rebel groups.

**Regional Guide**

*Etchmiadzin, Tbilisi*                                                                 *M. Karanian*

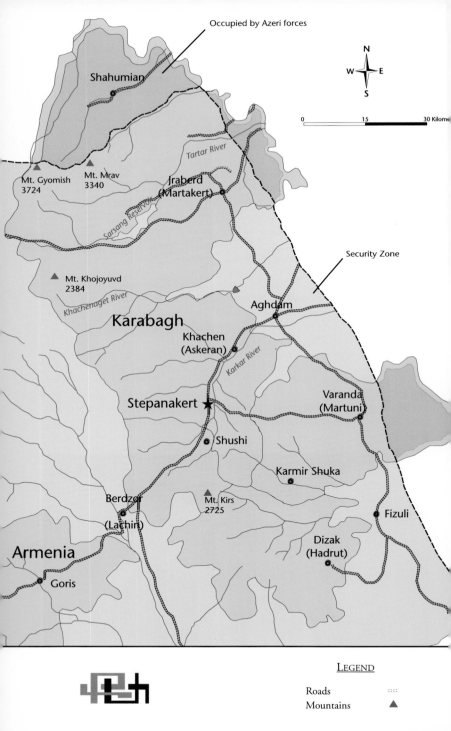

# Journey to Karabagh

*The soil itself was black and sticky, peeled back from the seed-trenches like asphalt. It has made these mountain villages into little Edens, and some of its fecundity has rubbed off on to the villagers themselves, helping to swell their high spirits.*

—Philip Marsden, *The Crossing Place*

Karabagh is a tiny Armenian state that is situated within the borders of the ancient Armenian province of Artsakh. Throughout ancient times, this lushly vegetated and mountainous region had been Armenia's easternmost principality.

As with many parts of historic Armenia, however, Karabagh's borders have been mangled over the centuries and it has been bounced back and forth between the competing imperial powers of the region. It has been sought as a prize and has been overrun by Arabs in the eighth century, by Turks in the eleventh century, and more recently by Persians and Russians.

The ongoing political misfortunes of this region are perhaps best indicated by the etymology of its name. Karabagh's name is either a mix of Persian and Russian meaning Black Garden, as is widely accepted, or it's an Armenian compound meaning the land of the Bagh. The Bagh, or Balayi, were a tribe of Armenians who lived in this area in ancient times. The Russians added the adjective Nagorno, which means mountainous, and dubbed the region Nagorno Karabagh. Most Armenians simply call it Artsakh, although the state is officially known as the Nagorno Karabagh Republic (NKR).

In 1920, Josef Stalin manipulated Karabagh's borders in a way that made it an Armenian enclave situated entirely within the Soviet republic of Azerbaijan, even though Armenia lay just six miles away. Stalin's intention, it would later become apparent, was to keep the various nationalities of the empire divided and too weak to challenge the center.

The Armenians of Karabagh never accepted this situation. By 1988, after suffering decades of misrule by the surrounding Azeris, the Karabagh government formally voted to secede from the union-the first such vote ever in the Soviet Union. Moscow intervened but was unable to put a stop to Karabagh's demands for independence. By December 1991 Karabagh had held a referendum and had declared its independence.

Azerbaijan responded militarily to this democratic affront and it attacked civilian targets throughout Karabagh and laid siege to the Armenian-populated city of Stepanakert. For the Armenians, the siege evoked memories of the genocide of 1915 and they fought feverishly for their survival. They eventually pushed the enemy forces back to Azerbaijan and established a security zone around Karabagh, as well. A ceasefire has been in force since May 1994 and the Western powers have spent the past several years trying to broker a peace deal between Azerbaijan and Karabagh.

Despite more than a decade of independence, the Nagorno Karabagh Republic is not yet an internationally recognized state. It sure acts like one, however. It maintains officially-registered representatives in the US, France, Russia and Armenia, despite a lack of diplomatic relations and it has a formal government consisting of an elected president and parliament. Karabagh restricts immigration, controls its borders, requires visas for foreign visitors and issues its own postage stamps. Karabagh has all the attributes of sovereignty, and for the purposes of tourism, travelers must treat it as an independent state. Accordingly, this chapter treats it as such, as well.

*Note about place names: The names of many places and streets have been changed during the past decade. This text therefore identifies all streets and towns by their new names, followed in parentheses by the prior name, whenever it's likely that confusion would otherwise result.*

## GETTING THERE

Getting to Karabagh can be a simple matter, as long as you start your journey in Armenia. There are no commercial flights in or out of the country but there is reliable ground transportation from points throughout Armenia. This is remote territory, and will require at least two full days of travel just getting in and out. Keep in mind that Karabagh is like a giant *cul de sac* off a main highway. You can't just pass through on your way to somewhere else. Spring, summer and autumn are the best times to visit. In winter, snow and ice at the higher elevations can obstruct roads and make it difficult to get around.

### Before You Go

A **passport** and **visa** are required of all visitors, except those with Armenian passports. Karabagh doesn't have official diplomatic relations with foreign states, and so there are no embassies abroad. To apply for a visa, go to Karabagh's Permanent Representative in Yerevan, Armenia (Tel. 52-64-28). You'll find it on the third floor of a government office building on 11 Moskovian Street, near the intersection with Abovian Street, and not too far from the Yeritasardakan metro station.

You can also apply for a visa at the office of one of Karabagh's representatives in the US, France, Russia, Lebanon and Australia. Contact information for the US office is listed in the *Travel Information* section below. As of 2002, however, these offices were not actually issuing visas, but were instead forwarding the applications to the Karabagh Representative in Yerevan. This office in Armenia is the only location where a traveler can take possession of a visa for Karabagh. You cannot obtain a visa at the Karabagh border.

*Photograph: Dadivank, M. Karanian*

Because of this, you absolutely must travel through Yerevan in order to reach Karabagh. Karabagh's only open border is with Armenia, so the only passage is through Armenia, anyway. Karabagh's border with Azerbaijan is closed and militarized and the two countries are hostile. There is also no direct transit from Iran.

Applying for a Karabagh visa is quick and easy. There's a short form that asks where you plan to stay, and why you wish to travel there. You can fill out the form in English, Russian or Armenian. The fee is $25 for a one-week visa, which you must pay in US dollars, and an additional tax of 1,000 dram (less than $2), which must be paid in Armenian currency. You also need two passport-sized photographs. The turnaround time for a visa is usually 30 minutes or less, making this perhaps the most efficient government office in all of Armenia. The office will also issue a 21-day visa on the day of application for $45 plus the 1,000 dram tax.

If you didn't bring spare passport photos with you from home, you can get some made nearby. For fast service, try the Photo Opera store at 1 Baghramian Ave. This same-day photo lab is located at the traffic circle near the Opera House, where Baghramian Ave. and Sarian Street intersect. It's 1,000 dram (less than $2) for four photos, which you can usually pick up in a couple of hours. For faster service, there's a photo lab on Moskovian Street, only one block from the Karabagh representative's office, where you can usually get four passport photos in only five minutes, also for 1,000 dram.

A Karabagh visa in your passport will bar you from any subsequent travel to Azerbaijan. If you already have an Azerbaijan visa in your passport you will face greater scrutiny during your passage to Karabagh. If you want to avoid having a Karabagh visa in your passport, tell the clerk before you apply. You may be able to have it attached with a paper clip instead.

*M. Karanian*                                                            *Vankasar Monastery*

## Travel Information

The latest information about conditions in Karabagh is available on the Internet from **www.artsakhworld.com** and from **www.artsakh.org**. Karabagh's government-run web site, **www.nkrusa.org**, is also helpful. Other news sources are listed in this book in the section on Armenia. The US Dept. of State posts travel advisories on its website at www.state.gov. The UK Foreign Office does the same, at www.fco.gov.uk. Karabagh maintains an office of representation in the US where you might find additional resources. Vardan Barseghian is the Representative. Write to him at the Office of the NKR in the USA; 122 C Street, NW; Suite 360; Washington, DC 20001 (Tel. 202-347-5166; Fax 202-347-5168) (E-mail: nkr-usa@artsakh.org).

## Getting There by Air

There are no commercial flights into Karabagh but it is still possible to fly in. Many tour agencies in Armenia, including **Sati Tours** in central Yerevan, can help you charter a private helicopter. The fare in 2002 was $2,500 for a round trip, but the 20-seat government-owned helicopter has to return to Yerevan the same day—the operator won't leave it in Karabagh overnight. These flights can be hazardous. There's a risk of mechanical failure, as well as the risk of getting shot down by enemy forces. Flying time is about one hour. Karabagh-based **Asbar Travel Agency** can also charter a helicopter for your group as part of a three-, four-, or five-day tour. Details are available on their website www.asbar.nk.am. Contact them at 25 Vazgen Sargsian (Yerevanian) Street, 3rd floor; Stepanakert, NKR. You can call them from the US using their Yerevan number (Tel. / Fax 374-1-28-65-10) (E-mail: travel@asbar.nk.am).

## Getting There Overland

The safest and easiest roadway into Karabagh passes through the Armenian town of Goris, and then through the so-called **Lachin Corridor**. Thanks to a new highway that links Karabagh and Armenia, this journey has been dramatically shortened. One can expect to travel by private car from Yerevan to Stepanakert, the capital city of Karabagh, in only about five or six hours. This is roughly half of the travel time of just a few years ago. And today the journey no longer requires a four-wheel drive automobile or long delays while bulldozers clear you a path amid the rocks and soil.

This corridor that the new road passes through is located between the Armenian town of Goris, and the Nagorno-Karabagh town of Shushi. It got its name during Karabagh's war of independence. International observers dubbed it a humanitarian corridor, and they attached the name Lachin to the corridor because this is the main town along the route. Today, Lachin is known by its original Armenian name, **Berdzor**. The mountainous region that it sits astride, and which had once been a mere corridor, has now been integrated into Karabagh. But habits die hard, and most foreign travelers still refer to the region as the Lachin Corridor.

The new roadway between Goris and Stepanakert is 90 km, and it has been re-engineered, widened, and re-paved all the way to Stepanakert, thanks to the massive financial support of Armenian-Americans through the Armenia Fund, USA,

Inc. The road is still unavoidably full of switchbacks and hairpin turns because of the mountainous terrain, and travel time is about two and one half hours.

There is also a passage to Karabagh through the **Kelbajar** region, which is north of the Goris to Stepanakert roadway. The road is in a military zone, however, and land mines are known to be present, so we urge you to stay away.

There are no major car rental agencies in Karabagh, but private drivers are plentiful. Ask around, and you'll be able to hire a driver for about $100 to $150 for a round-trip journey of two or three days. Negotiate the fare, as well as compensation for food and lodging, before departure. Your hotel can help you find a driver, or you can call one of the cab companies and make special arrangements, if you are unable to locate a reliable driver on your own.

For a less expensive alternative, travel by bus or minivan. Daily vans operate from the Kilikia Central Bus Station to **Stepanakert**. Departures are at 8 am and at 9 am. Travel time is roughly six hours, and the fare is 6,000 dram (about $12). From Hotel Shirak, a van departs daily at 7:30 am. Travel time is roughly six hours, and the fare is only 4,000 dram (about $8).

There are daily busses, as well, and they cost even less than the vans. These are the big red Intourist busses from the Soviet era. Travel times are dreadfully slow, sometimes 12 hours or more. They're uncomfortable, too, and we cannot recommend them. The one-way fare, however, is only 3,000 dram (about $6), so it's popular with the locals.

Travelers should arrive at the bus station or the hotel one hour before the scheduled departure of a van, in order to claim a good seat next to a window, or to get any seat at all—the seats get filled quickly. Sit on the right side of the van, where you'll have unobstructed views of Mt. Ararat. Bring a bottle of water, and some food, since you may be in the van for four or more hours before stopping. If you are susceptible to carsickness, take precautions before you reach the winding mountain roads that connect Goris to Stepanakert.

## After You Arrive

An immigration officer will check your visa and record your passage in a handwritten ledger. This stop is made near Berdzor (Lachin), the first town along the roadway into Karabagh. The driver will also be required to present his automobile and driving documents. This is the same routine that is followed in Armenia and Georgia, with one big difference. There are rarely any hassles or unnecessary delays at the Karabagh frontier. Car trunks are sometimes checked for contraband. But if your papers are all in order, you'll be sent on your way within a few minutes. If you don't have a visa, you will be turned back. Visas are not available at the border checkpoint.

There is no formal customs procedure here. Once you reach the capital, Stepanakert, however, you are required to register with the Karabagh Foreign Ministry. They'll give you travel papers that will list the towns or regions that you are allowed to visit, and you'll be warned to stay away from risky areas. Expect entry to be forbidden to regions near the Azeri frontier, or to any towns that formerly had Azeri populations. The Foreign Ministry is centrally located at 28 Azatamartikneri Street.

## LANGUAGE AND PEOPLE

Armenian is the primary language in Karabagh, although Russian is also popular. The people of Karabagh speak a unique dialect of Armenian, however, which can slow down translators. The population is roughly 144,000 according to the official estimates, of whom roughly 95 percent are Armenian. The remaining five percent of the population is mostly Russian, Greek or Assyrian.

## CLIMATE AND GEOGRAPHY

Karabagh is a mountainous land, and is heavily forested in many parts. Temperatures are much cooler here than they are in central Armenia, and there's a great deal more rain, too. Travelers should bring a sweater or sweatshirt even in the summer, and rain gear, too. The mountainous elevations frequently result in cold winters. Ice and snow on the roads can cause delays, and travel at night is frequently not advisable during the winter. Fog can also create hazardous driving conditions.

## SAFETY

By mid-2002, the terrorism of September 11 had not had any apparent effect upon the ability to travel to Karabagh. Officials have reported no new restrictions on travel throughout Karabagh, but there are still many that are in place because of Karabagh's hostile relations with neighboring Azerbaijan. Martial law remains in effect. See the "After Your Arrive" section above for more details. Despite all this, the streets of Stepanakert are peaceful and there are no areas that one must avoid at night.

*Berdzor Region*                                                                 *R. Kurkjian*

Towns that once had Azeri populations are polluted with land mines, and a bucolic-looking pasture could easily prove to be deadly if you walk through it. Visitors absolutely must stay out of deserted Azeri villages and towns, including the biggest of them, Aghdam, or risk death or serious injury. Stepanakert is safe. Elsewhere, you should generally walk only on streets and sidewalks or in areas that have been declared safe. Areas that are near the Azeri frontier are off-limits. There are still occasional violations of the 1994 cease-fire, and travel near the border is dangerous and prohibited.

## HEALTH

Health precautions for travelers in Karabagh are the same as in Armenia. Bring any special medications you reasonably believe you may need, including prescription medicines and fever reducers such as aspirin and ibuprofen. Bring antidiarrheal medicine such as Imodium ®, and check with your doctor about bringing antibiotics. Karabagh does not require proof of any immunizations in order to gain entry, but travelers should consult the health section on Armenia to learn about recommended vaccinations. The Centers for Disease Control can provide the most current medical information for travelers to Karabagh, and to the rest of the Caucasus (Tel. 1-888-232-3299) (Internet: www.cdc.gov/travel).

## MONEY

The local currency is the Armenian dram. The euro is also widely used, however. Some merchants may accept US dollars, but it will be tough to get change for denominations of $5 or higher. Visitors should change their dollars to Armenian dram before arriving in Karabagh, or use one of the half dozen officially licensed exchange offices that are located throughout Stepanakert. There are no ATM machines, and banking services are rudimentary. Wire transfers can be arranged at the larger banks, however, including **Artsakh Bank** which is located near Republic Square at the intersection with Sasuntsi David Street.

## TELEPHONE

From inside Karabagh, if you wish to place a call to someone located outside of Karabagh you must go to a special office, usually a post office, and request an international line. In Stepanakert, the Telecom Post is located on the upper part of Vazgen Sargsian (Yerevanian) Street. Calls to the US are roughly $4 for each minute. Calls to Armenia are much less expensive. Payment must be made in Armenian currency. There's a bank located two doors away if you need to exchange money.

From outside Karabagh, it can be difficult to place a call to someone located inside Karabagh. If you are in Armenia, you can place a call to Stepanakert by using the **country code 8-89322**, followed by the local five-digit telephone number. If you are calling Karabagh from anywhere else in the world, you cannot dial directly. Instead, you can gain access only by calling a special Yerevan trunk line, because all calls must be routed through Yerevan. Your call will be answered by an operator, who will then connect you to the local Karabagh phone number, but only if the person that you are calling is a subscriber to this special service. In addition to any long distance charges that you incur, the person you are calling will also pay a toll. Many international organizations use this service, which is known locally as a "Panasonic Line." Access numbers for the trunk line are: 28-07-01; 28-64-15; and 28-65-10, all preceded by the requisite (011) 374-1 prefix.

*Northern Karabagh*                                                    *R. Kurkjian*

## INTERNET

Access to the Internet while in Karabagh is something that we have always found difficult. Fortunately, some Internet cafes have opened, making access easier. **Arminco Ltd.** operates an access site from an office on the third floor at 25 Vazgen Sargsian (Yerevanian) St. They charge one dollar for each hour online. **Artsakhtel JSC,** operates on Hakopian St., at the intersection with Mamikonian Street. Their rate is 46 dram (eight cents) per minute, which is about $5 per hour. **Pandok Internet Café** is located on Mamikonian Street, and charges $1 for each hour online.

## MAIL

Letters and postcards sent to the US directly from Stepanakert's main post office generally arrive in about two or three weeks. Mail that is posted here will be routed first to Yerevan, where it is combined with Armenian mail and then sent to its final destination. The post is located on Hakopian Street, between Vardan Mamikonian Street and Vazgen Sargsian (Yerevanian) Street, and it sells its own Karabagh postage stamps for all mail and for collectors. The rate for letters to the US in 2001 is 250 dram (about 50 cents), and the rate for a post card is 170 dram (about 35 cents).

To send a letter to Karabagh, address it to the recipient, at the recipient's street address, in care of Artsakh State Post Office, Stepanakert. Then on the next three lines write: State Post Office; Moskovian #11; Yerevan, Armenia 375000. All mail destined for Karabagh must be routed through Yerevan.

Sergei Galandarian is a private dealer who sells stamps for collectors, and reports significant interest among foreigners. He is located at 21 Vazgen Sargsian (Yerevanian) Street, Apt.#3, Stepanakert (Tel. 4-36-77).

## MAPS

The only city map of Stepanakert that we know of, in any language, is the one we produced for this book on page 120. English-language wall-size maps of Karabagh exist but are difficult to find. Look for one in Yerevan before your journey at the Noyan Tapan bookstore on Republic Square or the Vernissage outdoor market, which operates on weekends.

## BOOKS AND TELEVISION

There are no English-language periodicals, and English-language books are a rarity. There's a public library located at 9 Vardan Mamikonian Street, but their 53,000 volumes are all in Armenian or Russian. Broadcast television is from Armenia and Russia, and there is also a local station that broadcasts for a brief time each day.

## FOREIGN OFFICES

There are no foreign embassies in Karabagh, but there is a tiny community of expatriates who might be helpful to business travelers who are interested in networking. The **Armenian Assembly of America** has a small office at 28 Azatamartikneri Street, Stepanakert (Tel.4-37-74) (E-mail: office@aaa.nk.am). Other large international organizations are: **Armenian Technology Group** (Tel / Fax 5-11-58) (E-mail: zakiyan@arminco.nk.am); **Catholic Relief Society** (Tel. 5-17-86); **Family Care** (Tel. 4-21-97) (E-mail: family@arminco.nk.am); and **International Committee for the Red Cross** (Tel. 4-37-70) (E-mail: icrcstenk@icrc.nk.am); **Medecins Sans Frontiers (MSF)**, Belgium MSF (Tel. 4-06-79) and France MSF (Tel. 4-18-90); and **OSCE** (Organization for Security and Cooperation in Europe Field Office) (Tel. 4-57-78) (E-mail: office@osce.nk.am).

# HOTELS AND PLACES TO STAY

Most of the comforts of the West have not yet reached this remote mountainous region. Many of the hotels don't have running hot water, for example. But you can still find some familiar comforts in Stepanakert, as long as you have a few dollars in your pocket. Indeed, Stepanakert and Shushi are the only places in Karabagh where you can find comfortable hotel accommodations. We recommend that you find your lodging in either of these towns, both of which make suitable departure points for any touring in Karabagh. You might be able to make an advance reservation by calling from Yerevan, but this really isn't necessary for a hotel unless you need several rooms for a large group.

Hotels outside the capital city will certainly disappoint all but the most seasoned and vigorous travelers. You should consider them only after first taking a look at them, and only when you cannot get back to Stepanakert. A more comfortable alternative in the remote areas might be to stay with a local family. Be sure to leave a gift of several dollars for their hospitality.

## Stepanakert

Stepanakert's newest and best rooms are at the **Lotus Hotel**. There's running hot water in every bathroom all day long, and the bathrooms themselves are modern and clean. Owner Satik Meneger built the hotel in 1998, and expansions have been underway ever since. In 2000, there were 24 rooms available with accommodations for 55 guests. **Amenities:** There's a color television and VCR in each room, a refrigerator in some, and a mix of private and shared Western-standard bathrooms. Facilities include a restaurant, bar, recreation room and a planned swimming pool. Laundry service is available. Single with shared bath $35; Double deluxe room $70. Walk to town in 15 minutes, or take a $1 cab ride. No handicapped access, stairs to all floors. 81 V. Vagarsbian Street (Tel. 4-38-82; or 4-16-20) (E-mail: lotus@nk.infostack.net). Please note that you may have difficulty getting through to Karabagh on e-mail.

The **Karabagh Hotel** has been a fixture of central Stepanakert since it opened in 1936. There's running hot and cold water only in the first floor bathroom, which is shared by all guests. Second floor guests carry water to their rooms in pails. Many of the rooms have been freshened up during the past couple of years, and the linens and blankets appear to be clean, and fairly new. The hotel is fine for someone who is flexible and doesn't expect anything more than a bed and a roof, but a stay of more than one night might prove tiresome, even at these prices. Single $3; Double $5. No handicapped access, stairs to all floors. Located on Republic Square next to the Parliament Building (Tel. 1-37-93).

**Guest Houses** are available as well, if you ask around. For the past several years, Nora Babayan has operated an informal bed and breakfast at her home near the center of town. She rents three rooms on the top floor of her private home, where guests share one bathroom. There are five twin-sized beds, a double bed, and there's

also a foldout couch in the common area. The entire place is impeccably clean and neat, and there's hot water all day long. Nora is vivacious and friendly, and most of her customers are referrals from past guests. The authors have stayed here each year since 1995, and highly recommend it. All prices, including the cost for laundry services and meals, are negotiable. Lodging typically costs about $15 per night for each person. Visitors should call from Yerevan before traveling to Karabagh to guarantee availability (Tel. 4-49-10). She is located at 11 Rubeni Street, near the residence of Karabagh President Arkady Ghukasian.

Two *dachas* operate near the Papik-Tatik monument at the northern edge of town, but are not recommended unless there's no alternative available. They are remotely located and a bit pricey. **Lavanda** *dacha* has an outdoor swimming pool and mountain views from the balconies. The rooms are new and clean. Single $60 (Tel. 4-19-59). **Lousabats** *dacha* also features extravagant accommodations, at least by local standards. We haven't seen the interiors of the rooms here, but the building appears to be impeccably maintained. Single $60; Double $120.

## Shushi

The 12-room **Hotel Shoushi** opened for business in 2001, making it the first hotel in town and the only one outside of Stepanakert that we recommend. It's located near the Ghazanchetsots Cathedral in the center of town, convenient to everything in Shushi. **Amenities**: Full-sized beds, and Western-standard bathrooms. Some of the rooms have a sofa and desk. Single $35; Double deluxe room $65. There's also e-mail and internet access and a Yerevan phone line. Breakfast included. 3 Amirian Street (Tel. 374-1-28-65-10 or 374-1-28-64-15) (E-mail: reservation@shoushihotel.com) (Website: www.shoushihotel.com).

## Distant Regions

In the southern town of Varanda (Martuni), the government-owned **Artsakh Hotel** offers one deluxe and nine regular rooms in the center of town. There's no hot water, and the baths are all shared. All accommodations: 1,000 dram (about $2). Located on the main square.

Up north in Jraberd (Martakert), the **Jraberd Hotel** offers 19 dark and Spartan rooms. There's only cold water, and it's only in a shared bath on the first floor. Each room has a balcony, but there aren't any views. Regular rooms 1,000 dram (about $2); Deluxe rooms 1,500 dram (about $3). Located on Azatamartikneri Street, which is also known as Lenin Prospekt.

## FOOD AND DRINK

If you are traveling outside Stepanakert, pack a lunch and a bottle of water, because you're not likely to be able to purchase a meal in the countryside. Your chances of finding a restaurant inside Stepanakert are much better, but you will probably still want to purchase fresh fruits, vegetables and bread from a market.

*Journey to Karabagh*

*Photograph: At the Shuka in Stepanakert, R. Kurkjian*

**Haik Pizza** serves pizza topped with *basturma*, which is spiced dried beef, and boiled eggs, as well as more traditional toppings. Pizza and a beer is about $3, which is expensive by local standards. Located at 1 Mkhitar Gosh Street, near Azatamartikneri Street and below Republic Square; **Green Bar** has been popular with foreign visitors ever since it opened in 1997. Located on Azatamartikneri Street, below Republic Square; **Express Bar** has outdoor seating on a porch high above the street, and sells light food. Located on Grigor Lusavorich Street; **Oasis Café** has outdoor seating at a sidewalk café, and is located just above Republic Square on Vazgen Sargsian (Yerevanian) Street. **Pandok Café**, at 24 Vardan Mamikonian Street, offers light food as well as beer and soda. **Tsitsernak Restaurant**, on upper Vazgen Sargsian (Yerevanian) Street, serves *khorovats*, *shish kebob* and local specialties.

The main **shuka**, or outdoor farmers market, is located on Baghramian Street, south of Republic Square, and is a great place to visit, even if you're not shopping. Vendors also sell farm produce throughout the town at shops, on the sidewalk, and even from the back of trucks. Fresh bread is plentiful and is available at most shops and it is a simple matter to locate bottled water and genuine Coca-Cola.

## SHOPPING

There's a gift shop called the ***Vernissage*** at 11 Vardan Mamikonian Street, where tourist souvenirs are available. Next door, artist Samvel Gabrielian operates a painter's studio where you will find some artwork for sale. **Penta Electronics**, where you can purchase a radio or just some fresh AA batteries, and a photo lab that sells color print film, are also on this city block. Across the street, on Pavlova Street, there are a dozen or more sidewalk vendors selling food, clothing, and assorted goods.

## GETTING AROUND

### Group Tours

The only practical way to tour Karabagh is with a private driver. Public transportation inside Karabagh is not reliable, and the delays would be unbearable for a tourist with limited time. There are several **group tours** that you can join which have departures from Yerevan. These tours will typically travel by mini van through Goris in southern Armenia, and then into Karabagh through the Berdzor Region (Lachin Corridor), past the town that is now known as Berdzor. Visa arrangements are sometimes left to the guests, so check this beforehand to be sure.

**Asbar Travel Agency** in Stepanakert can arrange tours for individuals or for groups of two or more people, by mini van or by helicopter. Because they are based in Karabagh, they are more likely to be familiar with Karabagh than an agency located in Armenia or the US. Asbar can also assist with hotel and visa arrangements, if you prefer to travel independently. Asbar Travel Agency, 25 Vazgen Sargsian (Yerevanian) Street, 3rd floor, Stepanakert. You can call them from the US using their Yerevan number (Tel. 28-56-10) (E-mail: travel@asbar.nk.am) (Internet: www.asbar.nk.am).

## Independent Touring

**Public transportation** into and out of Karabagh is convenient and easy. If you are independent minded and you prefer to avoid the group tours, you can easily make arrangements on your own. Mini vans and busses depart from Yerevan's Kilikia Central Bus Station every morning, and arrive in Stepanakert about six hours later. Refer to "Getting There" for departure times and fare information. The return trip out of Stepanakert is from the town's central bus station on Azatamartikneri Street.

Upon arrival in Stepanakert, it is a simple matter to hire a **private driver** to take you around. Many taxi drivers will agree to work for about 100 dram for each kilometer traveled. A flat rate of $20 for the day is also reasonable for traveling within Stepanakert. There are no meters in the taxis, and all fares should be nego-tiated in advance. Either agree on a flat rate, or pay by the kilometer. On longer journeys of several hours you should offer a few dollars extra, and buy the driver's lunch. Keep in mind that many drivers are unemployed professionals, and that your driver may be a physicist or an engineer.

We have found that **Yura Gasparian** is a safe and reliable driver who is knowledge-able about the local road conditions. He has lived in Karabagh all his life, and can be a big help in finding ancient sites. He operates a mini van that can seat about ten people, and a sedan that can carry three passengers (Tel. 4-49-10).

*Farmland in southeast Karabagh*                                                    *R. Kurkjian*

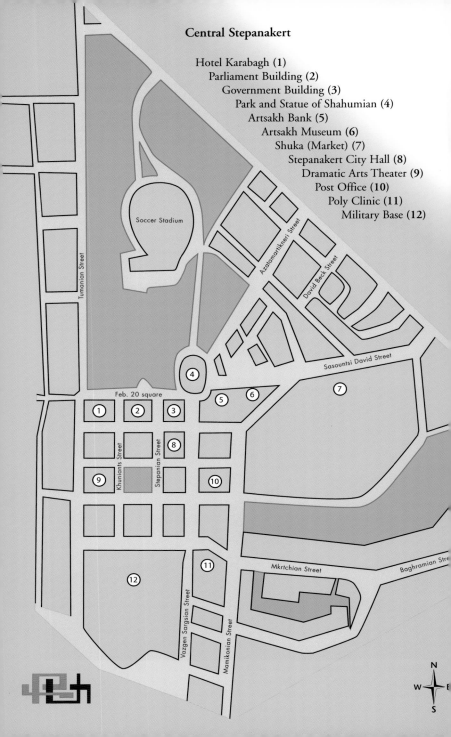

# Central Stepanakert

Hotel Karabagh (**1**)
Parliament Building (**2**)
Government Building (**3**)
Park and Statue of Shahumian (**4**)
Artsakh Bank (**5**)
Artsakh Museum (**6**)
Shuka (Market) (**7**)
Stepanakert City Hall (**8**)
Dramatic Arts Theater (**9**)
Post Office (**10**)
Poly Clinic (**11**)
Military Base (**12**)

# ATTRACTIONS/SIGHTSEEING

Visitors to Karabagh should use Stepanakert as a base from which to visit the surrounding regions. Stepanakert is the capital, it has the best lodging, and you can get to everything and still return that same day. Be sure to pack a lunch and bottled drinking water before journeying out to the country, since you're not likely to be able to buy what you want on the road. All travel times listed here are by private car from Stepanakert unless stated otherwise. But before you venture out, you'll want to take a look around town. **Note About Place Names:** The names of many places and streets have been changed during the past decade. This book therefore identifies all streets and towns by their new names, followed in parentheses by the prior name, whenever it's likely that confusion would otherwise result.

## Walking Tour of Stepanakert

Stepanakert is a small town, and travelers who enjoy walking will find that the best way to see this town is by foot. Starting from the Karabagh Hotel on Republic Square, which is the oldest operating lodge in all Karabagh, walk past the **Karabagh Parliament** building, and down a flight of steps to **Stepan Shahumian Park**. There are children's amusement rides and a café. There's also a Ferris wheel that offers superb views of the area, including a view of the famous monument of **Papik-Tatik**. The monument was erected in 1967, and an inscription on the back reveals its official name "We Are Our Mountains." Cross over to Azatamartikneri Street, which is actually a continuation of Vazgen Sargsian (Yerevanian) Street, and you can either walk to the monument in about fifteen minutes, or take a 500 dram cab ride.

Back at Republic Square, walk to the **Artsakh State Museum**, which is located just about 50 meters from the Square, at 4 Sasunstsi David Street. Here, an assortment of ancient artifacts and Christian manuscripts are on display in a strikingly unpretentious manner. There are also modern relics from World War II and from the events of the past decade, which, in the local nomenclature, is simply "our war." The building is open Monday through Saturday until 5 pm, or sooner if the handful of workers grow weary. Admission is free, but donations of a dollar or two are accepted. There's a **carpet factory** called "Artsakh Rugs" at 31 Azatamartikneri Street (just below Republic Square, next to Green Bar) that's worth a look. If you stop by on a weekday, you'll be able to see the craftsmanship in progress. The manager, Oleg Paghshian, says all tourists are welcome to stop by. You might even want to make a purchase, or place a custom order.

## Touring Throughout the Region

The **Berdzor Region**, which many foreign visitors still refer to as the "Lachin Corridor" because of its status as a humanitarian aid corridor during the Azeri siege of Karabagh in the early 1990s, is the region's link to Armenia. Travelers must pass through Berdzor even before reaching Shushi, and it is in Berdzor that you will find the fifth century monastery of **Tsitsernavank (Swallow Monastery)**. It is located in the Ahavni (Aghavnaget) River valley, which is accessible by turning off the main road near the customs checkpoint. Turn left at the bridge near the town of Berdzor (Lachin) and drive along the narrow road for about 45 minutes. Some scholars

*M. Karanian*          *Ghazanchetsots Cathedral, in Shushi*

believe the building may have existed in some form even earlier than the fifth century, as a pagan temple.

**Shushi** is the first major town in Karabagh that you drive past when you travel to Karabagh from Armenia. The topography is stunning, and the sheer cliffs that limit the expansion of the town also serve to insulate and protect it from outsiders. This small town is just 15 kilometers outside of Stepanakert, and it should be on every visitor's itinerary. Travel time is about 20 minutes.

There's a magnificent **Persian fortress**, which was built in 1724, and two working Armenian churches. There are a couple of mosques, too, but they are damaged from the war and are closed.

Shushi's history has been tragic. As many as 35,000 Armenians had lived in Shushi until 1920, when they were all either killed or expelled by invading forces from Turkey and Azerbaijan. Seven thousand Armenian homes were destroyed. Shushi's status as one of the region's leading cultural centers was also snuffed out.

The Armenians recovered Shushi in 1992, and it is still in ruins from the war. One of the large tanks involved in the battle now forms part of a monument located on the roadside between Shushi and Stepanakert. Don't photograph military sites. There's no express law prohibiting other photography, but police or security agents might stop you if you are walking around with a camera. Carry your passport, or at least a photocopy of it, so that you can identify yourself if you are stopped and questioned. You'll get a good view of Stepanakert from Shushi's high perch. It was from this same perch that Azerbaijan laid siege to Stepanakert during the war.

**The Ghazanchetsots Cathedral** in Shushi is a massive structure with a façade of white stone that dominates its surroundings. It's also known as the Cathedral of

*Shushi*                                                                    *R. Kurkjian*

Christ the Savior. The freestanding belfry that stands near the front entrance was built in 1858, a decade before construction was begun on the main church. The church has seen many uses over the years, not all of which have been religious. During the period of Azeri control of the town, beginning in 1920, the church was used a granary, as a garage, and finally as a munitions storehouse until May 9, 1992 when the Azeris retreated. The building was heavily damaged and its artwork was defaced. The Armenians have made extensive repairs during the past few years, however, and reconstruction was completed in 2000. This cathedral is one of 19 churches and monasteries throughout Karabagh that have been restored during the past decade. If you cannot pronounce its name, call it the Shushi Cathedral and you'll be understood.

**Kanach Zham** is another Armenian church located uphill from the Cathedral. This church is sometime called Karabaghtsots in honor of the farmers from Karabagh who built it in 1847. More frequently, however, the people of Shushi call it Kanach Zham, which translates to "green church." The origin of the name is logical, inasmuch as this church's domes were at one time painted green. The ruins of **Meghretsots Church** are also nearby. Only the eastern wall and two apses remain.

On the midpoint along the roadway between Stepanakert and Shushi there's a turnoff for **Karmir Shuka**. This road leads to a picnic grounds at **Skhtorashen**, where there is a 2,000-year-old tree that you can walk through. Perhaps more interesting, however, are the beautiful fields and pastures along the way, near Karmir Shuka. Travelers don't normally visit here, which is a shame because this bucolic region may be one of Karabagh's most beautiful areas. This road also passes the ruins of an ancient church. The fieldstone church is only about 20 feet from the side of the road, but trees and shrubs partially screen it from view. This is another of Karabagh's off-the-beaten-path antiquities, and we recommend that you visit.

The **Monastery of Amaras** is located south of Stepanakert in the **Varanda (Martuni) Region**, near the village of **Machkalashen**. Farmland and endless fields of wheat surround the complex, but a fortress of tall stone walls nevertheless surrounds Amaras. The unlikely sight of the walls betrays the painful history of this monastery. The monastery has been repeatedly plundered and rebuilt for the past 1,500 years. Its most recent brush with disaster was in 1992, when enemy forces briefly seized it. The oldest church at the complex was built by St. Gregory the Illuminator sometime around AD 310. The real claim to fame for Amaras comes from its connection with Mesrop Mashtots, the inventor of the Armenian alphabet. Mashtots taught here roughly 1,600 years ago. Not surprisingly, his teachings included the alphabet that he had just created. The monastery is the oldest in Karabagh, but the main church and the current focal point of the complex is a more recent addition. It was built in the nineteenth century. This rectangular church is constructed from white stone, and is named St. Gregoris, in honor of the grandson of St. Gregory the Illuminator. Travel time to Amaras is about two hours.

A **Statue of Monte Melkonian**, an Armenian-American who became a hero of Karabagh's war of independence, is located near the center of the town of Martuni, outside the city government building. There's a military hospital and a military base nearby, as well. A new religious center, the **Church of St. Nerses the Great**, is under construction. Diligent and persevering explorers will want to seek out the monastery of **G'Tichavank**, which is located in a remote region south of Martuni and west of Fizuli, in the Hadrut region. G'Tichavank dates to the thirteenth century and it stands today in disrepair.

The **Gandzasar Monastery**, which is located north of Stepanakert in the **Martakert (Jraberd) Region**, near the village of **Vank**, is another day trip that every visitor should consider. Construction of the church was begun in AD 1216, and the entire complex is protected by a high wall. The exquisite bas-reliefs on the exterior walls are unique, and have been compared to the elaborate inscriptions of Aghtamar, a church located in historic Armenia. Gandzasar's bas-reliefs depict the Crucifixion, Adam and Eve, and two ministers holding a model of the church above their heads, as an offering to God. The monastery was damaged during an Azeri bombing raid in 1991, and one building—the house of the Father Superior—was lost. The English language translation of the name Gandzasar is "treasure mountain," and to view the splendor of its architecture is to understand why. Some scholars and historians consider the monastery to represent one of the top masterpieces of Armenian architecture. Gandzasar is actively functioning today, and it is the seat of the **Archbishop of Artsakh** of the Armenian Apostolic Church. Travel time to Gandzasar is about two hours.

The town of **Askeran** is located about 12 km north of Stepanakert, in the region of **Khachen (Askeran)**, and is the site of a fortress that spans a shallow river and the major roadway, as well. Just north of town there's a war memorial on the left side of the road which features a large tank that was used to defend the region.

*Journey to Karabagh*

*Photograph: Kanach Zham in Shushi, M. Karanian*

Travel farther up this road to the **Vankasar Monastery** which stands a lonely vigil outside **Martakert**. This building is located on a sparsely vegetated hilltop just off the main road that links **Jraberd (Martakert) Region to Aghdam**, and it is visible from several kilometers away as one approaches by car. The tiny church is built of a cream colored stone, and it sits on a peak that is about 100 meters from a military radar and observation post. Because of this military post, government officials say that tourists are not welcome unless they have permission from the base commander, and that groups of more than three people are not likely to be admitted.

If you decide to visit, we urge you to get permission by going straight to the military post and identifying yourself as a tourist. Use extreme caution, and avoid landmines by walking only in designated areas. Hire a local guide or driver who can help you get permission. The military observation post occupies a house that had been the dacha (summer home) of a high-ranking Azeri official before the war. Ironically, locals credit this official with having repaired the church before the war. You are apt to see many wild rabbits, owls and other rare birds while you are there. The church is about 40 km from Stepanakert. Travel time to Vankasar is about one hour.

Visitors who are interested in learning about the people of Karabagh may also choose to continue up the road for about 20 km (travel time from the church is about 20 minutes) and visit the town of **Martakert**, which was the site of fierce fighting during the war. Today it is largely in ruins. Upon the approach to town there's a neat and orderly village of modern homes that was built with funding from Germany. On the horizon ahead of the main road a large Ferris wheel marks the location of the old town. There are only two major roads within Martakert. On Azatamartikneri Street (formerly Lenin Prospekt), the people of the town built a tiny **Historical Local Museum** in 1997, to replace the one that had been destroyed by enemy forces during the war. One large room in the museum is a portrait gallery featuring the images of local men and boys who were killed during the war. The museum is open weekdays from 8 am to 6 pm.

**Central Regional Hospital** is also nearby, in the center of town. The hospital's 250 bed capacity was reduced to about eighty after the war, but significant improvements have been made during the past two years. Walking from the ruined main wing of the hospital and into the new maternity ward is like walking along a timeline from the Soviet era and into the modern future. Elsewhere on the same road, the local people are rebuilding the church of **Surb Hovhannes Mkrtich**. This church is a new one, having been built in 1881, but it was destroyed during the war. Travel time from Stepanakert to Martakert is about one hour and twenty minutes. We recommend that you do not travel north of Martakert. The roads north of town will lead you dangerously close to the front line with Azerbaijan, which is militarized, and one risks being subject to hostile fire. If peace comes to the region, visitors will be able to travel to the **Yeghish Arakyal Monastery**, which dates to the fifth century, and to the **Yeritsmankants Monastery**, which was built in the modern era in 1691. Yegish Arakyal is located on the bank of the

Yeghsharakel River, which is a tributary of the Tartar River. Yeritsmankants, also known as the Monastery of Three Youths, is closer still to the border. Karabagh's northernmost region of **Shahumian** has been overrun by enemy forces and is now occupied by Azerbaijan. It is not accessible.

**Dadi Vank**, a stunning monastery that was built early in the twelfth and thirteenth Centuries, is unequaled in its mystery and majesty among the churches of Karabagh. According to legend, the monastery was originally established in the first century AD, but was destroyed and then rebuilt roughly 800 years ago. If the legend is true, then Dadi Vank would gain distinction as the oldest monastery in the Karabagh Region.

The complex consists of a three-story bell tower (AD 1334) and several other buildings, some of them with elaborate engravings and inscriptions on their walls. The largest of the buildings is the church of St. Dadi, which was completed in AD 1214. Its main altar is used daily by the local villagers, and it frequently displays an assortment of gifts and messages that they have left behind. On the outside of the southwestern wall, there's a bas-relief of a model of the church being offered to God. Below it there is an inscription, written in Armenian. It says, "I, Arzu Khatun, obedient servant of Christ…wife of King Vakhtang, ruler of Artik and all Upper Khachen, with great hopes have built this holy cathedral on the place where my husband and sons are laid to rest…. Done in 663 [AD 1214] of the Armenian calendar." Inside, fresco paintings adorn the larger walls.

To reach the monastery, drive northwest beyond Martakert (heading farther away from Stepanakert) through the village of **Kusapat** (9 km/20 minutes from

*Ancient church near Karmir Shuka*                                        *R. Kurkjian*

Martakert) and past the large village of **Getavan** (53 km/three hours from Martakert). Just after Getavan there is a military checkpoint, and the monastery is just a bit farther.

The road to Dadi Vank winds past the **Sarsang Reservoir** and along the **Tartar Canyon**. Sarsang is the largest body of water in Karabagh, and this is a great place to stop to rest when driving to Dadi Vank. This area is remote and forested, and the unlikely appearance of the ancient monastery adds to its mysterious charm. The best time to visit is in the summer, when you can go and still get back to Stepanakert before dark. The distance from Stepanakert is only about 133 km, but the poor and often unpaved roads extend the travel time to about four hours. Dadi Vank is in disrepair but its survival nonetheless is miraculous. West of the monastery, in the town of Tsar, another ancient religious site fared less well. The **Monastery of Tsar**, built in 1301, was deliberately destroyed by the Azerbaijan authorities during the Soviet era. The monastery was blown up, two thirteenth century chapels were razed to the ground, and the pride of Tsar, the Church of the Holy Virgin, was dismantled. The elaborately engraved stones of the church were used to build storehouses, and they are today visible in the foundations of barns built by the Azeris. The author Boris Baratov documented the destruction, both in words and photographs, in the book "A Journey to Karabagh: Paradise Laid Waste."

We recommend that you do not travel beyond Dadi Vank, into the region of **Kelbajar**, which is a military zone. The road from Kelbajar to the southern region of Lake Sevan in Armenia is poor even by local standards, and the journey is said to take at least five hours in a four-wheel drive vehicle. Military commanders may not allow you to pass, however, and even if they do the journey might not be safe because of the land mines in this area.

*R. Kurkjian*                                                    *Shepherd in Shushi*

**Journey to Karabagh**

The *best* resource for Armenia photography

Stone Garden Productions

888-266-7331   www.stonegardenproductions.com

# BOOKSELLERS

There are several large booksellers throughout the US that sell titles on Armenia, Karabagh and the Caucasus. Four of the largest-volume sellers in the northeast, listed alphabetically, are: the **Armenian General Benevolent Union (AGBU) Bookstore**, 55 East 59th Street, New York, NY 10022 (Tel. 212-319-6383) (Internet: www.agbu.org); the **Armenian Prelacy Bookstore**, 138 East 39th Street, New York, NY 10016 (Tel. 212-689-7810); **NAASR**, 395 Concord Ave., Belmont, Mass. (Tel. 617-489-1610); and **St. Vartan Bookstore**, Armenian Diocese, 630 Second Ave., New York, NY 10016 (Tel. 212-686-9893).

In the Los Angeles area, several privately-owned bookstores offer large inventories of books and music about Armenia in both English and Armenian. Listed alphabetically, they are: **Abril Bookstore** (Tel. 818-243-4112) (Internet: www.AbrilBooks.com); **Berj Books** (Tel. 818-244-3830); **Hye Keer Books** (Tel. 818-342-6624); and **Sardarabad Bookstore** (Tel. 818-500-0790) (Internet: www.Sardarabad.com).

# INTERNET SITES

There are thousands of websites devoted to Armenia and the Armenians. The sites that we have listed below are a handful of some of the most helpful sites and are a supplement to the web addresses that are found throughout the text of this book.

## Political, advocacy or benevolent organizations

Perhaps the most interesting is **ArmenianDiaspora.com** (organization of Armenians throughout the world); Other good sites are: **anca.org** (Armenian National Committee of America); **aaainc.org** (Armenian Assembly of America); **agbu.org** (Armenian General Benevolent Union); **Armenian-Genocide.com** (Armenian National Institute).

## Governments

The best of the government sites is **ArmeniaEmb.org** (Armenian Embassy in the US); Also try: **Artsakh.org** (Karabagh's Ministry of Foreign Affairs); **Gov.am** (official site of the Republic of Armenia); **NKR.am** (Ministry of Foreign Affairs); **arminco.com/embusa/consul.htm** (official site of the US Embassy in Armenia); and **ArtsakhWorld.com** (Karabagh's historic sites).

## News and Information

The most comprehensive site, and one which deserves a bookmark on your computer, is **EurasiaNews.com** (extensive information and news about Armenia and Eurasia); Other top sites include: **ArmeniaGuide.com** (travel information); **Armenia.com** (portal to other sites); **Asbarez.com** (online edition of the daily newspaper); **FreeNet.am** (e-mail service); **Groong.com** (news service); **Hayastan.com** (portal to other sites); **Hyelink.com** (portal to other sites); **HyeGuide.com** (the arts, travel, history and other interesting subjects, as well as a portal to other sites)

## Non-profit and NGO sites

**ArmeniaFund.org** (humanitarian organization); **ArmenianVolunteer.org** (volunteer activities); **LocalHands.org** (public health in Karabagh); **lcousa.org** (Land and Culture Organization); **habitat.org/GV** (Habitat for Humanity's Global Village program in Armenia); **peacecorps.gov/countries/armenia/index.cfm** (Peace Corps); **pyunic.am** (Armenian association for the disabled)

## Commercial Sites

**Narek.com** (largest online seller of music gifts and books); **Zoryan.org** (book seller and links to other sites); **KurkjianImages.com** (stock photography).

# Take the threeway to Yerevan.

Yerevan flights increased to three times a week.

# HOTEL
# ARMENIA

*Enjoy the **luxury***
*and the **convenience***
*in the **heart** of Yerevan*

Photo © Robert Kurkjian

**1 Amiryan St. Yerevan**
**Armenia 375010**
**Tel: (3741) 599-000**
**Fax: (3741) 599-001**
**www.hotelarmenia.com**

# EPILOGUE

A large tent, big enough for a grand show, had been erected near the entrance to the village of Lusarat, and its canvas walls were flapping to the beat—the loud beat—of traditional Armenian music and dancing.

If you had walked north from this tent for a couple of hundred meters, you would have walked across a sandy and rock-strewn moonscape that is littered with the scrubby undergrowth of wild grasses. You would have seen a barren land that is no different today than it was when the Armenians first walked here roughly three thousand years ago. You would have seen that there is nothing here. And that everything is here.

We had traveled to this site dozens and dozens of times during the past several years, but we had rarely ventured into this nearby village. Each time, we had made it to within a couple of hundred meters of the village, and so it was today, as well. We could have seen the village if we had just looked to the left. But the sun was setting, and we were photographing an ancient monastery. So we didn't look. We might as well have been a world away—in the world of Khor Virap.

Khor Virap is the name of the ancient Armenian monastery into whose world we had surrendered ourselves to yet again. Despite having made hundreds of images of the monastery with Mets Masis (Mt. Ararat) in the background, the mystique of the site compelled us to return to make more. So we set our cameras upon tripods, and we clicked away.

This monastery's complex of buildings was built in the seventh century, and religious services are regularly conducted there today. Many foreigners are surprised to discover this. But what else, besides prayers, should one expect to see at a religious site, the Armenians might ask.

The site is stark, its simple beauty is even startling, but Khor Virap is not imposing. There are no road signs directing one to the monastery, nor is there a sign announcing its presence. The gate is locked each day at 5 pm. This is not a grand tourist destination, but it is one of the most significant Christian sites within the modern Republic of Armenia.

On this evening, however, the revelry of the circus tent eventually lured us away. We could faintly hear the celebrants above the din. We turned away from the ancient brown stones of the monastery, and walked along the barren land that separated the monastery from the town. With each step, we felt ourselves drawn closer not just physically, but also spiritually.

When we arrived at the tent, we could see that there were hundreds of people celebrating the wedding of two of the village's young people. They were inside the tent, and they were spilling out all over. They were doing line dances. They were offering toasts of Armenian cognac. They were enjoying feasts of khorovats and

*continued on page 151*

dolma, and friendship and festivity. We had just left the black and white world of ancient Armenia, and had stumbled upon the colorful and dynamic world of a festive village.

During several years of travels throughout Armenia and Karabagh, we had photographed hundreds of villages, and thousands of villagers. And quite a few city folk, too. But this was the first time we had stumbled upon a wedding fiesta at full volume. We thought we would take a couple of photographs of this traditional Armenian party, and we asked if they would permit us. It wasn't necessary for us to ask permission more than once. Armenians love to be photographed! And they love to entertain guests.

The reception that we received was no different from any of the countless others that had preceded it in other towns and villages across Armenia. The Armenians welcomed us to their nominally private event, despite having only known us for a few moments. They offered us food. They foisted drinks upon us. And they did this without hesitation.

We attempted to decline their hospitality. We made photographs of two young children, and we started to leave. We had inadvertently become the centers of attention at someone else's wedding, and we felt uncomfortable about this.

A couple of guests stood in our way.

"Where do you have to go? When do you have to be there?" Our explanations were not accepted.

Stay, they pleaded. Sit, eat, drink. The villagers were sincere and they were emphatic. They wanted us to stay. So we accepted their invitation.

*Continued on next page*

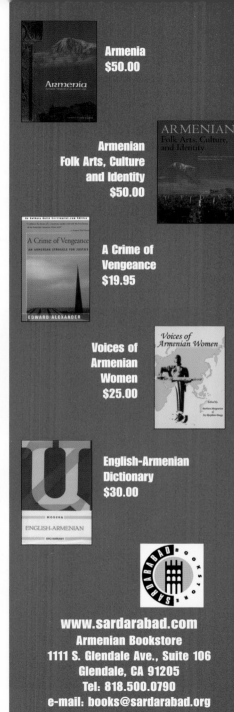

We drank some Armenian brandy, followed by Armenian coffee. We ate some pastries. We told some stories, and we listened to plenty more. We made new friends, for the simple reasons that the Armenians were jovial, and there was no reason not to be friends.

The only thing that was asked of us was that we return, and allow them to serve us lunch, or coffee, or whatever they had. They asked that we return and visit with their families, sleep in their homes, share in their lives.

We wondered how it was possible for such ordinary village people to be so kind, so friendly, so generous. We looked around and saw again that there was nothing here. We wondered how the villagers could give so much, when it was so plain to us that they themselves had nothing.

We left. And we returned. And we left again.

And we saw that they had everything, and that everything was here.

# APPENDIX

# MAJOR HOLIDAYS

Most businesses and offices are closed on these dates. Holidays are recognized by both Armenia and Karabagh, unless noted otherwise in parentheses.

NEW YEAR'S, DECEMBER 31 THROUGH JANUARY 2

This is perhaps the most joyous of the Armenian holidays and is marked by feasts, gatherings of family and friends, and the exchange of gifts. Neighbors and even strangers are welcomed into the home. Most businesses and offices are closed all three days.

CHRISTMAS DAY, JANUARY 6

Armenians celebrate the birth of Christ according to the Old Julian calendar, on January 6. This holiday is religious, and has not been commercialized

INDEPENDENCE DAY (KARABAGH), JANUARY 6

Commemorates Karabagh's declaration of independence in 1992. Karabagh's referendum on independence was held December 10, 1991.

WOMEN'S DAY, MARCH 8

This holiday is a holdover from the Soviet Union.

DAY OF MATERNITY AND BEAUTY, APRIL 7

This is a new holiday in Armenia, which celebrates not only mothers, but also all women. This holiday is partly redundant of Women's Day.

EASTER, (VARIES)

ARMENIAN GENOCIDE MEMORIAL DAY, APRIL 24

This is the most somber of national holidays. Tens of thousands make pilgrimages to the Genocide memorial, Tsitsernakaberd (Fortress of the Swallows) where they lay flowers at the eternal flame. Armenians here and around the world mourn the 1915-1923 slaughter of 1.5 million of their countrymen, and the destruction of their 3,000 year-old homeland. Shops and offices are closed, and many Armenians attend solemn church services.

SHUSHI LIBERATION DAY (KARABAGH), MAY 8

Recognizes the day in 1992 that the Karabagh army recovered Shushi, thereby ending a several-months-long siege of Stepanakert by enemy forces.

VICTORY AND PEACE DAY, MAY 9

This holdover holiday from the Soviet Union commemorates the conclusion of World War II.

ST. VARDAN'S DAY, MAY 26

Commemorates Vardan Mamikonian's battle against Persia in AD 451, which preserved Armenia's Christian status. Also known as Vardanants, which is a term used to describe the wars between Armenia and Persia in which Armenian fought for freedom of religion.

FIRST REPUBLIC DAY (ARMENIA), MAY 28

Also known as Independence Day, recognizing the first Armenian republic's independence in 1918.

CONSTITUTION DAY (ARMENIA), JULY 5

Commemorates Armenia's adoption, by plebiscite in 1995, of the national constitution. Businesses and stores remain open.

INDEPENDENCE DAY (ARMENIA), SEPTEMBER 21

Also known as Re-establishment Day, recognizing the Republic of Armenia's independence in 1991.

EARTHQUAKE VICTIMS COMMEMORATION DAY (ARMENIA), DECEMBER 7

Recognizes the victims of the 1988 earthquake. Most businesses and stores remain open.

**Appendix**

# REFERENCES AND FURTHER INFORMATION
## BOOKS

### History and Politics

*Armenia at the Crossroads*, Joseph R. Masih and Robert O. Krikorian (Harwood Academic Publishers, 1999)

*The Armenian People, from Ancient to Modern Times*, Richard G. Hovannisian, ed. (St. Martin's Press, 1997)

*Armenia, The Survival of a Nation*, Christopher J. Walker (St. Martin's Press, 1980)

*The Challenge of Statehood: Armenian Political Thinking Since Independence*, Gerard J. Libaridian (Blue Crane Books, 1999)

*The History of the Armenian Genocide: Ethnic Conflict from the Balkans to Anatolia to the Caucasus*, Vahakn N. Dadrian (Berghahn Books, 1995)

*A History of the Armenian People, Pre-history to 500 AD* (Vol. 1), *1500 to Present* (Vol. 2), George Bournoutian (Mazda Publishers 1993, 1994)

*Looking Toward Ararat: Armenia in Modern History*, Ronald Grigor Suny (Indiana University Press, 1993).

### Karabagh

*The Caucasian Knot: The History and Geopolitics of Nagorno-Karabagh*, Levon Chorbajian, Patrick Donabedian, and Claude Mutafian (Zed Books, 1994)

*The Medieval Art of Artsakh*, H. Hakobian (Parberakan, 1991)

### Georgia

*Georgia: A Sovereign Country of the Caucasus*, Roger Rosen (Odyssey, 1999)

*The Making of the Georgian Nation*, Ronald Grigor Suny (Indiana University Press, 1994)

### Wildlife Guides

*A Field Guide to Birds of Armenia*, Martin S. Adamian and Daniel Klem, Jr. (American University of Armenia, 1997)

### Literature

*Black Dog of Fate*, Peter Balakian (Basic Books, 1997/Broadway Books, 1998)

*A Captive of the Caucasus*, Andrei Bitov (Weidenfeld and Nicholson, 1993)

*The Crossing Place*, Philip Marsden (Harper Collins, 1993)

*Forty Days of Musa Dagh*, Franz Werfel (1936)

### Photography

*Fragile Dreams: Armenia*, Antoine Agoudjian, (Actes Sud, 1999) 80 pp. Quality soft cover, black-and-white.

*Journey to Karabagh: Paradise Laid Waste*, Boris Baratov (Lingvist, 1998), 184 pp. Hardcover, full color.

*Out of Stone: Armenia-Artsakh*, Robert Kurkjian and Matthew Karanian (Stone Garden Productions, 1999), 184 pp. Hardcover, oversized, vibrant color.

*Photograph: Carpet weaver in Karabagh, R. Kurkjian*

# T U F E N K I A N
## Heritage Hotels

### LORI REGION

Planning to open in May 2003, the 34 room luxury Avan Dzoraget Hotel will be located beside the rushing Debed River in the Lori region—a land of wonderful mountain landscapes, ruins of medieval fortresses, and some of Armenia's most beautiful monasteries. The hotel and restaurant accommodate events for up to 80 people.

### LAKE SEVAN REGION

In July 2002, the first Tsapatagh Tourism Complex facilities will open. The Avan Marak Tsapatagh is a mid-priced two-floor lodge occupying a restored historic stone barn (marak), and is perfect for conferences and gatherings of up to 80. The Restaurant Zanazan, located in a renovated historic school with balconies overlooking the lake, seats 100.

### YEREVAN

This stunning 14-room hotel is located in a quiet residential neighborhood 10 minutes above the city center. With single, double, and suite rooms, it is the perfect choice for those seeking luxurious accommodations and an environment rich in the design of Armenia. Panoramic views of Yerevan, majestic Mt. Aragats and the breathtaking countryside are provided from all floors.

## Tufenkian Heritage Hotels…

is a network of luxurious properties in Armenia that combine great design, comfort and service, providing its guests with the richness of experiencing a revived Armenia—its culture, its village life and the natural beauty of its countryside. Guests can visit Armenian craftsmen at work, observing and learning the crafts of carpet-weaving, yarn-spinning, knitting, lace-making, cooking, iron-working, stone-carving and more. Visitors will make their contribution to the cultural and economic reawakening of Armenian villages by staying at a Tufenkian Heritage Hotel, participating in local festivals and fairs, buying the locally-made crafts at Tufenkian Craft Centers and enjoying other activities steeped in local traditions.

**347.1.543.122 voice**
**347.1.547.877 fax**

**tufenkian.am**
**tufhosp@arminco.com**

# PHRASES

## Greetings

| | |
|---|---|
| Hello | *barev* |
| Hello (polite) | *barev dzez* |
| How are you? (familiar) | *vonts es* |
| How are you? (polite) | *vonts ek* |
| Fine, thank you | *lav em, shnorhakalootyoon* |
| Very good | *shat lahv* |
| Very bad | *shat vaht* |
| What's up? (slang) | *eench kah?* |
| I'm tired | *hoknats em* |
| I'm sick | *heevand em* |
| I'm happy | *oorakh em* |
| Goodbye | *tstesootyoon* |
| What's your name? | *anoonut eench eh?* |
| Please | *khundrem* |
| Yes | *ayo* |
| No | *voch, cheh (colloquial)* |
| Goodnight | *baree geesher* |
| Have a good trip | *baree djanapar* |
| Father | *hayr* |
| Mother | *mayr* |
| Brother | *yeghbayr* |
| Sister | *kooyrik* |
| Friend | *unker* |
| Grandmother | *tatik, metz mayr* |
| Grandfather | *papik, metz hayr* |

## Getting by

| | |
|---|---|
| I | *yes* |
| You (polite, plural) | *dook* |
| You (familiar, singular) | *du* |
| I want | *oozoom em* |
| I don't want | *chem oozoom* |
| I know | *eemanoom em* |
| I don't know | *chem eemanoom* |
| Who | *ov* |
| What | *eench* |
| When | *yerp* |
| Where | *vortegh, oor* |
| Why | *eenchoo* |
| How | *eenchpes* |

## Traveling

| | |
|---|---|
| Hotel | *hyooranots* |
| Room | *senyak* |
| Bathroom | *zoogaran* |
| Elevator | *verelak [leeft]* |
| Restaurant | *djasharan* |
| Café | *srdjaran* |
| I'm hungry | *sovats em* |

| | |
|---|---|
| I'm thirsty | *tzarav em* |
| Postage stamp | *namakaneesh* |
| Letter | *namak* |
| Post office | *[post]* |
| Store | *khanoot* |
| Laundry | *lvatskatoon* |
| Telephone | *herakhos* |
| Telephone number | *herakhosee hamar* |
| Open | *bats* |
| Closed | *pak* |
| Bus | *avtoboos* |
| Bus Station | *avtoboosakayan* |
| Airplane | *otanav* |
| Airplane | *otanavakayan* |
| Subway | *[metro]* |
| Street, road | *poghots, djanaparh* |
| Highway | *mayrooghee* |
| River | *get* |
| Lake | *leedj* |
| Movie | *[kino]* |
| Luggage | *djambrook* |
| Taxi | *[taxi]* |
| Left | *dzakh* |
| Right | *ach* |
| Straight | *oogheegh* |
| Stop | *kangnee* |
| Up | *verev* |
| Down | *nerkev* |
| Here | *aystegh* |
| There | *ayntegh* |
| Time | *zham* |
| What time is it? | *zhamuh kaneens eh?* |
| Today | *aysor* |
| Tomorrow | *vaghuh* |
| Day after tomorrow | *vaghuh che myoos or* |
| Yesterday | *yerek* |
| Hot (weather) | *shok* |
| Cold (weather) | *tsoort* |
| Cheap | *ezhan* |
| Expensive | *tang* |
| Money | *pogh* |

## Food

| | |
|---|---|
| Bread | *hahts* |
| Food | *kerakoor, hahts (colloquial)* |
| Barbecue | *khorovatz* |
| Yogurt | *matzoon* |
| Cheese | *paneer* |
| Sugar | *shakaravaz* |
| Rice | *breendz* |
| Meat | *mees* |
| Fish | *dzook* |
| Chicken | *hav* |
| Lamb | *vochkhar* |

| Beef | tavar |
|---|---|
| Egg | dzoo |
| Green vegetables | kanachee |
| Tomato | lolik [pomeedor] |
| Cucumber | varoong |
| Apricot | tziran |
| Spicy | kutzoo |
| Hot | tak |
| Cold | pagh |
| Sweet | kaghtsur |
| Salt | agh |
| Pepper | beebar |

## Beverages

| Water | djoor |
|---|---|
| Cold water | saruh djoor |
| Milk | kaht |
| Tea | tey [chai] |
| Coffee | soordj |
| Armenian coffee | Haykakan soordj |
| American coffee | Amerikyan soordj |
| Yogurt beverage | tahn |
| Beer | garedjoor, [peeva] |
| Wine | geenee |
| Red wine | karmir geenee |
| White wine | spitak geenee |
| Vodka | oghee |

## Colors

| Red | karmir |
|---|---|
| Orange | narundjagoyn |
| Yellow | degheen |
| Green | kanach |
| Blue | kapoyt |
| Brown | surdjagoyn |
| Black | sev |
| White | spitak |
| Dark | mook |
| Light | bahts |

## Numbers

| One | mek |
|---|---|
| Two | yerkoo |
| Three | yerek |
| Four | chorse |
| Five | heeng |
| Six | vets |
| Seven | yot |
| Eight | oot |
| Nine | eenuh |
| Ten | tas |
| Twenty | kuhsahn |
| Thirty | yeresoon |
| Fourty | karasoon |

| Fifty | heesoon |
|---|---|
| Sixty | vahtsoon |
| Seventy | yotanasoon |
| Eighty | ootsoon |
| Ninety | eenneesoon |
| One hundred | haryoyr |
| Thousand | hazar |
| Many, a lot | shaht |
| A few | keech |

## Weekdays

| Monday | Yerkooshahptee |
|---|---|
| Tuesday | Yerekshahptee |
| Wednesday | Chorekshahptee |
| Thursday | Heengshahptee |
| Friday | Oorpaht |
| Saturday | Shahpaht |
| Sunday | Keerahkee |
| Every day | ahmen or |

## Sightseeing

| Mountain | sar |
|---|---|
| Church | yegheghetsee, zham |
| Monastery | vank |
| Fortress | bert |
| Hill | bulur |
| Stone | kar |
| Stone cross | khatchkar |
| Road | djanapar |
| City | kaghak |
| Village | gyoogh |
| House | toon |
| Building | shenk |
| Museum | tangaran |
| Camera | loosankarchakan [aparat] |
| Film | [plyonka] |

## Questions/Statements

| Stop | kanghnee |
|---|---|
| Sit | nustee |
| Come | aree |
| Look | nahyee |
| Let's go | gnatseenk |
| Go | gnah |
| How do I get back to Yerevan? | |
| | Vonts em gnoom Yerevan? |
| Where are you going? | |
| | Oor es gnoom? |
| Do you know? | Geetes |
| Where is? | Oor eh? |
| What is? | Eench eh? |
| How much does this cost? | Sa eench arzhee? |

# INDEX

162

# MILEAGE

## Distances from Yerevan in Kilometers / Miles

Artashat . . . . . . . . . . . . . . . . . . .29 / 18

Ashtarak . . . . . . . . . . . . . . . . . . .20 / 12

Dilijan . . . . . . . . . . . . . . . . . . .109 / 58

Echmiadzin . . . . . . . . . . . . . . . .20 / 12

Garni . . . . . . . . . . . . . . . . . . . .48 / 30

Goris . . . . . . . . . . . . . . . . . . . .250 / 155

Gyumri . . . . . . . . . . . . . . . . . . .120 / 75

Hrazdan . . . . . . . . . . . . . . . . . .50 / 31

Jermuk . . . . . . . . . . . . . . . . . . .175 / 106

Khor Virap . . . . . . . . . . . . . . . .55 / 34

Sardarapat . . . . . . . . . . . . . . . . .60 / 37

Sevan . . . . . . . . . . . . . . . . . . . .55 / 38

Sisian . . . . . . . . . . . . . . . . . . . .217 / 135

Spitak . . . . . . . . . . . . . . . . . . . .101 / 63

Stepanakert . . . . . . . . . . . . . . . .360 / 224

Stepanavan . . . . . . . . . . . . . . . .157 / 98

Tsaghkadzor . . . . . . . . . . . . . . .68 / 44

Yeghegnadzor . . . . . . . . . . . . . .122 / 76

Zvartnots . . . . . . . . . . . . . . . . .15 / 11

## Distance from Stepanakert in Kilometers / Miles

Dadi Vank . . . . . . . . . . . . . . . .133 / 87

Goris . . . . . . . . . . . . . . . . . . . .90 / 60

Jraberd (Martakert) . . . . . . . . . .60 / 40

Karmir Shuka . . . . . . . . . . . . . .55 / 38

Khachen (Askeran) . . . . . . . . . .18 / 12

Shushi . . . . . . . . . . . . . . . . . . .22 / 15

Sourenavan . . . . . . . . . . . . . . . .40 / 27

Yerevan . . . . . . . . . . . . . . . . . . .360 / 224

# ABOUT THE AUTHORS

**Matthew Karanian** was born in the US and has lived and worked in Armenia for several years as a writer, a photographer, and a professor of law. Matthew graduated with a degree in international law from Georgetown University. He has worked in the US as a trial lawyer and in the Republic of Georgia as a Caucasus specialist for Georgetown University's Institute for the Study of International Migration. He has traveled extensively throughout Armenia, Georgia, Karabagh and Turkey and his writings about each of these lands have been published in the US, UK and Canada.

**Robert Kurkjian** is an environmental scientist and photographer who was born in the US. He has lived and worked in Armenia and Karabagh since 1995, as a professor of environmental studies and as a research director at the American University of Armenia. Robert has done extensive research throughout Armenia and the US and he earned his Ph.D. in geochemistry from the University of California, Santa Cruz. He has studied photography in both New York and Los Angeles. Photographs from his extensive travels throughout Armenia, Karabagh, South and Central America, Europe and Asia have been published in numerous books and periodicals worldwide. He and his wife Alina were married in the ancient Armenian town of Shushi and they have two young sons, Aren and Vahn.

*"Bari Djanabarh"*
*Enjoy the Armenian*
*Experience...*